Day by Day

WITH THE PSALMS

Douglas Cleverley Ford

The Bible Reading Fellowship

DAY BY DAY
WITH THE PSALMS

Published by
The Bible Reading Fellowship
Peter's Way, Sandy Lane West
Oxford OX4 5HG
ISBN 0 7459 2975 3
Albatross Books Pty Ltd
PO Box 320, Sutherland
NSW 2232, Australia
ISBN 0 7324 0950 0

First edition 1996
10 9 8 7 6 5 4 3 2 1 0

Acknowledgments

The Alternative Service Book 1980 copyright © The Central Board
of Finance of the Church of England.

The *Revised Standard Version* of the Bible, copyright © 1946,
1952, 1971 by the Division of Christian Education of the
National Council of the Churches of Christ in the USA.

Extracts from the Book of Common Prayer of 1662, the rights in
which are invested in the Crown in perpetuity within the United
Kingdom, are reproduced by permission of the Crown's
patentee, Cambridge University Press.

Extracts from the *Authorized Version* of the Bible (The King James
Bible), the rights of which are vested in the Crown, are
reproduced by permission of the Crown's Patentee, Cambridge
University Press.

New English Bible, © 1970 by permission of Oxford and
Cambridge University Presses.

A catalogue record for this book is available
from the British Library

Printed and bound in Slovenia

Contents

A note from the editor

Douglas Cleverley Ford's *New Daylight* notes on the Psalms are much loved by his readers, and we have had many requests to publish them in a more lasting form. So we have done so, and in *Day by Day with the Psalms* you will find a large selection of these notes. Some of them look at the same Psalm more than once, and as we look at it in a slightly different way, we shall understand its meaning more deeply.

Shelagh Brown
Commissioning Editor

Introduction

The book of Psalms in the Bible is a book of religious poetry. More exactly, lyrical poetry. That is to say, poetry which expresses the feelings of the writer, not about anything and everything in general, but—in the case of the Psalms—the experience of life drawn out by the unfailing awareness of the divine presence come what may, be it rough or smooth.

So the book of Psalms is not a uniformly tidy book. It has ups and downs, neat, orderly arrangements and also rough places not easy to negotiate. Nor can the various Psalms be dated with any degree of certainty, nor the precise conditions under which they were inspired.

The Psalms grew out of life, and life as we know it is never smooth for long. So the experience of God which they share with us is fragmentary, earthy and human. But as a result we can come alongside the Psalms. We can feel them, sing them misand sigh over them. Sometimes we knit our brows in puzzlement and sometimes we even shake our heads in doubt.

The Psalms are distillations of life—its joy, its wonder, its laughter, its pain, its loneliness and its fear. They are about living and about dying. It is no wonder they have lasted so long. They have never worn out and they never will. So be patient with them, sometimes reading them out loud and learning bits off by heart.

It would be possible to produce a book on the Psalms which drove potential readers away if they didn't happen to be academics. Let there be no mis-understanding. There is a proper place for learned works on the Psalms. Some of these volumes have their place on my bookshelves and they are well worn.

But my aim in this book is to attract the attention of ordinary people to the Psalms so that they may be nourished spiritually by them. This accounts for the illustrations sprinkled throughout the book, some of them homely and some of them lifted out of my experience. The aim of this book is to help the Psalms to address our own individual and contemporary condition, and above all to sharpen and deepen our awareness of the real presence of God in the bitter-sweet knocking about which we know as life.

So pick up this book on the Psalms and read it. Not all at once, but in bits and pieces—not omitting to complete your action with prayer.

Douglas Cleverley Ford
Lingfield, September 1995

Praise and Glory

How is it that we have a world? How did the universe come about? The answer popularly given is that the world is compounded of matter and energy. Everything that exists derives from these two basics acting and reacting together and evolving into a multitude of shapes and sizes and functions. There is a truth in this but when we go on to inquire where these originate we are given the answer: 'Chance. They came into being by chance.' Which of course is tantamount to confessing 'We do not know', the name for which is agnosticism. One of the consequences of this for people in general is meaninglessness, a dreary, hopeless reaction to life.

The Bible is different and the Psalms are different. They maintain that *God* is the author and sustainer of all that exists, including ourselves. The opening words of the Bible fix the groundwork of its viewpoint. 'In the beginning God.' The world, the universe, is not floating on chance and nothing. It is grounded on God, the eternal God, who does not have a beginning and will not have an end. The consequence of this belief is *praise and glory*. All we see and all we have is grounded in God and all we shall be is secured in God. We therefore praise God, and because we praise him we are witnessing to our faith as distinct from agnosticism. Where praise and glory are evident faith is evident, where praise and glory are lacking faith is lacking. All of this means that praise and glory must occupy a prominent place in our worship as they do in the Psalms, and those artists, poets, architects and musicians who adorn the praise and glory are contributing to the maintenance of the faith.

Psalm 95 sets the key: 'O come, let us sing to the Lord; let us make a joyful noise to the rock of our salvation, let us come into his presence with thanksgiving, let us make a joyful noise with songs of praise!' (RSV)

Prayer

Lord, I lift up my heart to add to the great volume of praise that goes round the world from all who love you. For that perky robin which perched on my fork handle as I dug the garden, for the glory of the woods in autumn—striking with their ravishing colours, for the whole world of nature, so rich, so vast and so full of wonder, and for what you have given me, home, friends, worthwhile work and above all my faith. All we have, all we are, all we can ever be derives from you the Great Creator, the Great Redeemer and the Great Lover of ordinary people, as I am. Praise to your most glorious name. Amen.

Properly rooted

And he shall be like a tree planted by the water-side: that will bring forth his fruit in due season. His leaf also shall not wither: and look, whatsoever he doeth, it shall prosper.

In spite of the beating it took in October 1987 in the great storm, the willow tree in my garden is still there, less a few branches and the foliage a little thinner perhaps, but strong, upright and graceful.

I planted it (with more luck than judgment) in the right place when thirty years ago I carried it, then a sapling, from the nursery next door. We haven't a stream in our garden but parts of it are more damp than others, so my willow tree, rooted there, has never lacked moisture. Its leaves have never withered through drought.

Now your day today, and my day, is not going to be rooted in the right place unless we find some place in it for prayer as best we can. Otherwise in spite of all the rushing about we do (equally if our activities are restricted for some reason), we shall 'dry out'. By this I mean anxiety, fretfulness, maybe even bad temper, or depression will take over and we shall not be the strong, upright and graceful tree we could be. Prayer causes the day to be properly rooted.

So get down on your knees (arthritic sufferers excused) and start by thanking God for something. No excuses please! There is always something. That you can read this (with or without glasses) . . .

that you have friends? (and perhaps a job?) . . . that the birds still sing . . .

Then confession. 'Lord I am sorry, I am not all I might be, I admit it, but you have promised to forgive me and help me to do better. I believe you.'

Then intercession, for other people who are in need, simply naming them, not telling God what to do! Then prayer for the day and what has to be done in it.

Simple? Yes, of course it is—and so was my planting of my willow tree in the proper place. But the result is striking. Prayer is the proper place to root each day.

A resolution

I will fix on a time and place for prayer each day, and stick to it.

The glory of God

The heavens tell out the glory of God, the vault of heaven reveals his handiwork. One day speaks to another, night with night shares its knowledge, and this without speech or language or sound of any voice. Their music goes out through all the earth, their words reach to the end of the world.

When this note is read I would like to think the sun is shining, the sky a resplendent blue, a gentle breeze from the south is carrying warmth and freshness; but I can't arrange it! The weather may be wet, muggy and windy. That will be a pity because I would like to picture my reader drawn out of doors as if by a magnet, stretching arms and legs, throwing back the head and exclaiming out loud, whether anybody is at hand to hear or not, 'O what a *glorious day!*'

I wonder if our religion ever makes us erupt with such feelings? Not all the time, that is impossible, but sometimes? If not, there is something wrong with it. I once knew a lady who was a most dedicated Christian, earnest and worthy but oh so drab, not in her dress but in her demeanour. There seemed to be no glory in her faith, no buoyancy, no laughter, no slack, everything about her was taut and serious.

Psalm 19 reminds us of the glory of God; the heavens proclaim it, even the night sky with its myriads of myriads of stars cries out the message—God's works is glorious. So does every day, ever night; the world over the music of God's creation is heard from the North Pole to the Southern Seas.

Will I be revealing any glimpse of this glory as I go about today? Or will I be a drab, dull Christian, so that those who meet me will be tempted to exclaim, 'No thanks, I have enough troubles of my own'? What a pity! What a travesty of the light, even the lightheartedness, the Christian should show.

Prayer

Lord, give me grace to be cheerful today and reflect something of your glory, even if it rains.

The praise of God

Judge me O Lord my God according to your righteousness: and let them not rejoice over me. Let them not say in their hearts 'We have our wish': let them not say 'We have destroyed him.' Let those that rejoice at my hurt be disgraced and confounded altogether: let those that lord it over me be clothed in shame and dishonour. But let those that long for my vindication shout for joy and rejoice: let them say always that the Lord is great who takes such delight in his servant's good. And my tongue shall speak of your righteousness: and of your praise all the day long.

Here is a man on whom someone has 'done the dirty'. You don't know how this feels? Then skip today's reading. It has nothing for you. But whoever wrote Psalm 35 knew only too well. He longed that he, or they, be disgraced and confounded altogether. And not only that, he wanted those who had ganged up against him to be covered in shame and dishonour. And he prayed God that this might happen! Were those worthy or unworthy prayers? Well, God can sort out our prayers. He has a dustbin for the bad ones.

But look! This furious man on his knees prayed for something better than the mere discrediting of his attackers. He wanted the people who longed for the vindication of the rightness of his cause to have a case for testifying to the greatness and goodness of God. He wanted his enemies overthrown so that God would be praised through the event. It was the praise of God that was his heart's desire.

A prayer

Lord, you know my heart; I am not vindictive. But I am jealous for the establishment of right, and for your greatness to be praised.

The form of praise

O clap your hands together, all ye people: O sing unto God with the voice of melody. For God is high, and to be feared: he is the great King upon all the earth.

The other day I saw a little girl given a doll. It was her birthday. She could scarcely believe her eyes—a beautiful doll with pink cheeks, golden hair, a sky-blue dress. Words failed her (not that she had many anyway), but she danced up and down and clapped her hands. She was overjoyed, and the expression of her joy was spontaneous.

The Psalmist bids up clap our hands because 'God is high, and to be feared: he is the great King upon all the earth'. Are we likely to do this? Isn't it a bit much? But some Christians these days use a form of worship which the critics label 'happy-clappy'. Who can quarrel with this, provided it is spontaneous and genuine? The danger arises when it is forced, and when only that form of expression is counted to be real, heart-felt worship. Much depends on one's temperament.

My father-in-law (long since dead) told me how as a young man, he was cycling in the highlands of Scotland. Not a soul came in sight for mile after mile. At last there appeared a solitary man, walking towards him.

'Nice day,' said my father-in-law, hoping for some response. It came.

Looking at him in the eye the lonely walker said, 'I ken that,' and marched on.

Rather a dour Scot, that one. Could you imagine him clapping his hands in church?

The Hebrews weren't dour. They clapped. And we should all praise God according to our different tempera-ments. So long as we do praise, the form doesn't matter. For some it will be Bach's Mass in B Minor, for others Taizé music.

A prayer

When I clap my hands (rather rare)
When I sing with a voice of melody (rarer still)
Accept my heart's desire to praise you, the great King over all the earth.

The Church

Walk about Zion, go round about her, number her towers, consider well her ramparts, go through her citadels; that you may tell the next generation that this is God, our God for ever and ever. He will be our guide for ever.

When you read this Psalm you have to imagine a sightseeing party and a guide with them; perhaps on a visit to Westminster Abbey or Canterbury Cathedral. And the guide says, 'Look at that! Look at that carving, and those buttresses! And the glass in those windows! And it has all been here hundreds of years, surviving all manner of calamities.'

And then ask yourself why it is we sing this Psalm on Whit Sunday. It is because the Church was founded on that day—Pentecost. Look at it, the Psalm in effect says, think how it has survived. It has never been rubbed out, not by the Romans, nor the pagan hordes from northern Europe, nor the Muslims, nor the Turks, nor the Japanese, nor the Chinese, nor the communists, nor the nationalists, nor the secularists, nor the hedonists. Of course there have been setbacks—some almost wiping it out—but the Church is still with us, numerically strong altogether though weak in some places.

At the present time the Church is coming in for a good deal of criticism. Some of it deserved. But don't write it off, don't desert it. Why not? Because God owns it. God inhabits it. It is his Zion. It cannot be destroyed because God cannot be destroyed. God is eternal so the Church is in touch with eternity. See how our reading today ends, not with towers and ramparts but with God for ever and ever, and he will be our guide into eternity. Make sure then we honour his dwelling place.

Walk about Zion, go round about her, number her towers, consider well her ramparts.

Prayer

Lord bless our local church and make it a place where you are known.

Our stronghold

Walk about Zion, go round about her, number her towers, consider well her ramparts, go through her citadels; that you may tell the next generation that this is God, our God for ever and ever. He will be our guide for ever.

Picture the inhabitants of a city, long-besieged, streaming out when the siege was lifted, to look at what was still standing. Look at the towers! they haven't been destroyed! See how the ramparts have stood up to the battering! What a story we have to tell our children! Zion, God's dwelling place, may be attacked *but it cannot be obliterated.* Yes, this is the God we acclaim, and will do for ever and ever.

No, we can't pinpoint the historical occasion, but does it matter? Our Zion, our Jerusalem, is the Church of God. It is not perfect. It never has been perfect. There are some disgraceful periods in its long history. But it is God's dwelling place; no, not his only dwelling place, but his special dwelling place. And remember this. God does not only choose perfect places in which to dwell, otherwise he would never look at your heart or mine.

There may be a fashion these days to despise the Church. Don't go in for it. God has chosen it; this is all that matters. It is not perfect but it can boast many saints, and look what art, music and learning it has inspired! What is more, it has withstood all the decrying, disdaining and destruction aimed at it.

Why? Because the Spirit of the living God has made it his humble dwelling place, and no one can destroy him.

A prayer

Lord, I thank you for the Church, warts and all—You founded it, the apostles built it up, and it has withstood a thousand knocks. Through the Church, Lord, directly or indirectly, I came to know you, and trust you, and be guided by you. Give me grace to do so today.

The water of God

You tend the earth and water it: you make it rich and fertile. The river of God is full of water: and so providing for the earth you provide grain for men. You drench its furrows, you level the ridges between: you soften it with showers and bless its early growth. You crown the year with your goodness: and the tracks where you have passed drip with fatness. The pastures of the wilderness run over: and the hills are girded with joy. The meadows are clothed with sheep: and the valleys stand so thick with corn they shout for joy and sing.

In the south-east of England, where I live, we are conscious of rain, not in the way they are in wetter parts, but either because in the lovely summers here it always seems to rain on the wrong days—for example just when we have an outdoor fête arranged; or, to the detriment of our gardens, there is insufficient rain, and then the Water Board forbids us to use our hoses and sprinklers! This is about as far as our thinking goes. We are not conscious, as we should be of *God's rain*, because we cannot do without it. Even I know this in my little sphere; for all my efforts in our last dry summer with watering-can and hose (when allowed), nothing would bring my garden on till we had some steady downpour of God's rain. The great truth is, we live by reason not only of our own efforts (yes, we do work hard!) but on God's provision. Without that we are nowhere.

Prayer

Lord, thank you for the sunshine and the rain, and for your wonderful bounty.

God's face

God be merciful unto us, and bless us: and shew us the light of his countenance, and be merciful unto us; That thy way may be known upon earth, thy saving health among all nations. Let the people praise thee. O God: yea, let all the people praise thee. O let the nations rejoice and be glad: for thou shalt judge the folk righteously, and govern the nations upon earth . . . Then shall the earth bring forth her increase: and God, even our own God, shall give us his blessing.

Here is an adolescent boy who has acted stupidly and landed himself in trouble; and since no one lives to himself he has caused trouble to others as well. And now he has to face his father. He dreads the meeting. But surprisingly he sees no hostility in his father's eyes, no hard lines around his mouth, instead an openness to him. At once his fear fades though he knows quite well that his father strongly disapproves of what he has done. But the light in that face changes the entire situation, it changes him—the boy.

In Psalm 67 we pray that God will shew us the light of his countenance. Perhaps this is half of our trouble. We do not see God as he really is. We see him as remote, dispassionate and stern. But God is our friend. The first in the Bible to believe this was Abraham, which is why he is important. And blessings followed as a result of that faith.

Psalm 67 longs that God's way with us should be known by all peoples everywhere for this would make for the health of humanity. Praising God for what he is heals our sores, then peace begins to dawn, and maybe even pros-perity (v. 6).

We would do well to begin each day with a *Te Deum*. 'We praise thee O God: we acknowledge thee to be the Lord. All the earth doth worship thee: the Father everlasting . . .' (I say these words on the way to the bathroom every morning.)

A stable family

God be merciful unto us, and bless us: and shew us the light of his countenance, and be merciful unto us; That thy way may be known upon earth: thy saving health among all nations. Let the people praise thee, O God: yea, let all the people praise thee. O let the nations rejoice and be glad: for thou shalt judge the folk righteously, and govern the nations upon earth. Let the people praise thee, O God: let all the people praise thee. Then shall the earth bring forth her increase: and God, even our own God, shall give us his blessing. God shall bless us: and all the ends of the world shall fear him.

When a couple are married in church (using the Prayer Book service), immediately following the pronouncement by the minister that they are man and wife, and his blessing added, they stand up and a Psalm is read—most likely our reading for today. The minister walks to the holy table and the couple follow him there and kneel down. So the very first thing they do together as man and wife is to pray together. Will it be the first and the last time?

Some years ago a phrase became current in the churches: 'The couple that prays together stays together.' May I make a practical suggestion? Family prayers are not easy to organise nowadays and people feel self-conscious about them. Why not a prayer said once a week when the family meets for Sunday dinner or whatever is its substitute? A grace could be extended into a prayer, and the prayer could be the reading of this Psalm keeping the memory of the wedding alive. Perhaps all might join in the Lord's Prayer at the end.

My brother used to have a weekly prayer like this with his wife and family. Even the dog attended. The dog was very quiet till the Lord's Prayer was reached, which he knew signalled the end. Then he went and stood by the door wagging his tail, because he knew the Sunday walk would be coming soon.

No, we needn't be too solemn about it, but couples and families ought to pray together sometimes, asking for God's blessing. Simple, but very effective.

A prayer

Lord, add your blessing to our family.
Bless us each one wherever we may be.

A place for all

Thy solemn processions are seen, O God, the processions of my God, my King, into the sanctuary—the singers in front, the minstrels last, between them maidens playing timbrels: 'Bless God in the great congregation, the Lord, O you who are of Israel's fountain!' There is Benjamin, the least of them, in the lead, the princes of Judah in their throng, the princes of Zebulun, the princes of Naphtali... Because of thy temple at Jerusalem kings bear gifts to thee... Let bronze be brought from Egypt; let Ethiopia hasten to stretch out her hands to God.

Everybody loves a procession. On occasions of state, people line the streets to watch and, high above, windows are crowded with faces. Televisions are not switched off that day.

Today's reading from Psalm 68 tells of a procession hundreds of years ago, long before the era of television, but the excitement was the same then as now. Here was a procession into the Jerusalem temple, giving praise to God for a great victory for Israel. In imagination, we can see how the procession is made up: 'the singers in front, the minstrels last, between them maidens playing timbrels'. We can make out what they are singing. 'Bless God in the great congregation, the Lord, O you who are of Israel's fountain!' But look now at the tail end of the procession. There are people from Egypt and Ethiopia, way outside Israel, carrying objects of bronze for their offerings. God wants us all to join in his praises, wherever we come from and whatever colour our skin is.

A prayer

Lord, save me from racial prejudice,
and from class prejudice,
and from occupational prejudice.
Let me be open to all,
as you are open to all,
even to me.

Festivals

O sing joyfully to God our strength:
  shout in triumph to the God of Jacob.
Make music and beat the drum:
  sound the lute and the melodious harp.
Blow the ram's horn at the new moon:
  and at the full moon for our day of festival.
For this was a statute for Israel:
  a commandment of the God of Jacob.

Shophar, the Hebrew word here, does mean a ram's horn, but I have to confess that I like the Prayer Book version better: 'Blow up the trumpet in the new-moon.' There is something about a trumpet. And there is that marvellous phrase in 1 Corinthians 15: 'And the trumpet shall sound and the dead in Christ shall rise first.' Then the seven angels sounding the seven trumpets in the Book of Revelation. All so stirring! Perhaps a ram's horn is stirring. I have never heard one. But it is the metal of the trumpet that makes it ring out.

Be all this as it may (and you can skip it if it bores you) note that the priests had to blow the ram's horn to initiate the Passover festival. It used to be a joyful occasion. The Hebrews observed regular festivals in their worship marked by the calendar. They were commanded to observe them and they were not dreary. There were drums, lutes and harps. The point is we shall have a false idea of what God is like, and what should be our response to him, if we never rise above prayers for deliverance from our troubles,

which are indeed bad enough. We need lifting out of them, however, and God is the great deliverer, and our form of worship ought to show that we rejoice in him. So blow up the trumpet (sorry! ram's horn) in church sometimes and observe the festivals as they come round. If nothing else, the human spirit needs variety.

A prayer

*Lord, I don't possess a trumpet or a ram's
  horn;
and if I did I could not blow hard enough
  to raise a sound out of it;
but I will observe the festivals,
and I will sing with the wind I have.*

We must sing

O sing unto the Lord a new song: sing unto the Lord, all the earth. Sing unto the Lord, and praise his name: be telling of his salvation from day to day.

Wouldn't it be wonderful if instead of reading the above words we all sang them! Think of it, hundreds and hundreds of people today right across the land and overseas all singing! Because the Psalms were written for singing. Some of them even have instructions attached about the tune. And they have become the songs of the Church. The Church has always been given to singing, to music and to bell-ringing.

People cannot, however, be made to sing. Singing has to come up from the heart. We need to have something to sing *about.* And anyone who has really heard the gospel of Jesus Christ, and trusted his/her life in consequence has precisely that. And how splendid if we know some hymns by heart, and not only the old ones but some of the modern ones as well. Sing them then, sing them out loud if you profess to be a Christian.

I like to sing in the garden when I am cutting the grass and somehow to sing outdoors amid the wonders of God's creation seems appropriate.

Let the heavens rejoice, and let the earth be glad: let the sea make a noise, and all that therein is. Let the field be joyful, and all that is in it:

then shall all the trees of the wood rejoice before the Lord.

Here is a picture of the whole creation praising God, and I joining in their company. Does this all sound comic? If you overheard me trying to sing now, though I was once a choirboy, you might think so. But I will hazard a guess, we shall do more to commend the gospel of our Lord by always being cheerful than by moralizing. Read verse 2 again, 'be telling of his salvation from day to day'. We do that when we have a song in our hearts and sometimes sing out loud with our throaty voices.

A prayer

We praise thee, O God: we acknowledge thee to be the Lord. All the earth doth worship thee: the Father everlasting.

from the Te Deum

Wonder

Wonderful are thy works! Thou knowest me right well; my frame was not hidden from thee, when I was being made in secret, intricately wrought in the depths of the earth.

A short while ago I had to pay a visit to the doctor. No, nothing serious, so you needn't be sorry for me! You know what it is like; I was shown into a waiting room and that was a true description. I waited. And I became bored. The magazines on the table didn't interest me.

And then my eye caught a small boy, aged about six, in the opposite corner of the room with his mum. He was bored. Then all of a sudden he spotted an aquarium in another corner of the room. It was lit up and had little fish swimming about. He was entranced and dragged over a chair to look at it more closely. I could see his face. It was a picture of wonder. There was wonder in his eyes, wonder in his movements. He called over to his mother to share his wonder. She tried but without enthusiasm. As I sat there waiting I reflected on what a fundamental gift wonder is. It is the root of wisdom. More than that it is the soil in which belief in God begins to grow. Without wonder the thought of God is not born. With it, it never dies. Last May I watched the man who helps me in my garden cup his hands round an iris in full bloom. He is not a religious man in any conventional sense but I overheard him say to himself, 'Cor blimey, look at that! Now it can't just

have happened. There must be some planning behind it somewhere.'

Wonder then at the world of nature. Wonder at the marvel of the birth of a human being. The Psalmist knew the meaning of wonder. I guess you could see it in his eyes. God has given us wonder so that we should know him.

Prayer

Lord we praise you for your wondrous creation. Give us eyes to see.

The mighty God

Bless the Lord, O my soul! O Lord my God, thou art very great! . . . Thou didst set the earth on its foundations, so that it should never be shaken. Thou didst cover it with the deep as with a garment; the waters stood above the mountains. At thy rebuke they fled; at the sound of thy thunder they took to flight. The mountains rose, the valleys sank down to the place which thou didst appoint for them. Thou didst set a bound which they should not pass, so that they might not again cover the earth.

Is our God too small? This Psalm points to the great God who made the world. It carries our thoughts back to God as Creator, reflecting his mighty works as set out in Genesis, chapter 1. When I kneel down to pray today, and you kneel down, this is the God before whom we are coming—the great and mighty one.

This means we must approach with reverence. We cannot tell God what he should do for us, or for *his* world, or for *his people*. And if we complain about our lot in life in his presence—and better that than not praying at all—we shall have to 'eat humble pie' in the end. 'O Lord, I am sorry. You are great and I am small and of no reputation!'

Yet the mighty God hears our prayers; we, they, are not too small for his attention. Have you ever boasted of a friend in high places? Someone who could do for you what no ordinary person without influence could do? *But he can.* And the mighty God is like that. A friend in high places! What a description of God! But if we really believe it we shall manage today with far more confidence.

A faith for today

Lord, thou art great and doest wondrous things, Thou God alone. And yet thou dost have respect unto the lowly; And that includes me.

A therapeutic religion

Bless the Lord, O my soul: O Lord my God, how great you are! ... You water the mountains from your dwelling on high: and the earth is filled by the fruits of your work. You cause the grass to grow for the cattle: and all green things for the servants of mankind. You bring food out of the earth: and wine that makes glad the heart of man, oil to give him a shining countenance: and bread to strengthen his heart.

The suggestion has been made that this psalm was sung as a temple hymn, probably at the New Year festival. Possibly, it would certainly be appropriate, but it must have originated in some one person's heart and mind when lifted up out in the open air before some scene of natural beauty. Poetry stems from individuals, not from committees.

What the Psalm does is to remind us of God in nature—God responsible for nature, not God the same as nature. This Psalm is based on Genesis chapter 1: 'God created the heavens and the earth'. What it does for us is to turn us away from ourselves to what we might call 'fresh-air religion', and this is therapeutic, for it saves us from ourselves. This is part of God's purpose in providing such a world, filled with so many wonderful things. The Creator is the Redeemer and the Redeemer is the Creator.

As I write this, on a mild autumn day, the pink late afternoon sunshine is lighting up the tall silver birch tree in my garden. But it appears not as silver today, but as a brilliant golden mass of leaves, almost breath-taking in its beauty. I want to stand by my study window and just gaze and gaze. Yes, my books, my papers and my prayer desk focus my religious devotion, but the result will be a narrow piety if I do not get outside to revel in the wonders of God's creation and praise him for them.

Thanksgiving

Thank you, Lord, for the beauty you have let me see.

God's creatures

Thou makest springs gush forth in the valleys; they flow between the hills, they give drink to every beast of the field; the wild asses quench their thirst. By them the birds of the air have their habitation; they sing among the branches. From thy lofty abode thou waterest the mountains; the earth is satisfied with the fruit of thy work. Thou dost cause the grass to grow for cattle, and plants for man to cultivate, that he may bring forth food from the earth, and wine to gladden the heart of man, oil to make his face shine, and bread to strengthen man's heart. The trees of the Lord are watered abundantly, the cedars of Lebanon which he planted. In them the birds build their nests; the stork has her home in the fir trees. The high mountains are for the wild goats; the rocks are a refuge for the badgers.

As I write this a blackbird is singing his head off in the silver birch tree just outside my study window. Because his song is out in the open we do not realize how powerful it is. Had he perched inside the house I should have had to plug my ears. But the birdsong is meant to be heard by other birds at a distance. All this the author of Psalm 104 would say is the design of God and the Creator. The birds are his and he has provided for them, and for the cattle, the wild goats and badgers. And we are bracketed with birds and animals as far as the Creator's provision is concerned; wine to make our hearts glad and oil to polish up our faces. Well, this is not quite how we would express it! But let us not miss the point. The Bible talks about God's provision whereas we talk about Nature's provision and leave God out; or else assume that God and Nature are the same which is definitely not what the Bible teaches.

The world of Nature certainly is wonderful. Modern television programmes reveal the wonders as never before but we must not deify nature. It is God's creation and the animals are God's creatures and it is our special duty *as human beings* to praise God for his creation.

A prayer

Lord, I think you for that blackbird and all the rich variety of nature that you have given us. Praise be to you the wonderful Creator.

God the provider

Thou dost cause the grass to grow for cattle, and plants for man to cultivate, that he may bring forth food from the earth, and wine to gladden the heart of man, oil to make his face shine, and bread to strengthen man's heart. The trees of the Lord are watered abundantly, the cedars of Lebanon which he planted. In them the birds build their nests; the stork has her home in the fir trees. The high mountains are for the wild goats; the rocks are a refuge for the badgers. Thou hast made the moon to mark the seasons; the sun knows its time for setting ... Man goes forth to his work and to his labour until the evening.

I have come to the country late in life; almost all my working life has been in central London. Now I am retired and I love my garden. I thank God for it. And shall I ever forget the first April when the various shades of green as the new foliage opened out almost took my breath away.

The trouble about living in built-up areas is that we can miss the beauty of nature. We half think that our food comes from man-made factories. But the truth is, the towns live because of the country. Everything we have derives from the good earth which God has given us. Yes, that is our faith. God is the provider and not only of the bare necessities of life, but of beauty too.

Read again today's verses. Note what are mentioned. Grass, cattle, trees, birds, wild goats, badgers... Also food to strengthen us, and wine to cheer us up. And the moon and the sun. How we should lift up our hearts in thanks and praise for all of this. Could we perhaps say our prayers sometimes out of doors?

An act of praise

Bless the Lord, O my soul, and forget not all his benefits.

Fresh-air religion

O Lord, how manifold are thy works: in wisdom hast thou made them all; the earth is full of thy riches. So is the great and wide sea also: wherein are things creeping innumerable, both small and great beasts.

I can't believe Psalm 104 was composed indoors. I can't believe it was written in a library or even in a church. I think it must have come to the Psalmist sitting high on a range of hills with the sea in the distance. The wind was blowing through his hair, his eyes were captivated by the clouds scudding across the blue sky, and not far away was the tinkling sound of a waterfall tumbling over the rocks. His heart was lifted up, and with a vibrant faith in the living God, he started to sing praises to the God whose handiwork all this loveliness was.

Yes, of course there is a place for church, stained glass windows and all, to keep our thoughts away from the world outside to concentrate for a while on God and his worship. There is a place too for the cloistered cell, though I personally am not very good at that kind of thing. What this Psalm does is to remind us of the worth of what I will call 'fresh-air religion'. It has a proper place and its essence is wonder, wonder at the beauty and prodigality of God's provision. Nothing stingy here, nothing second-class, nothing uniform. Its variety cries aloud. Fresh-air religion releases us from narrowness, from being turned in on ourselves and growing 'nervy' in consequence. It is therapeutic. So get out into the country if and when you can, and read this Psalm. Or better still, have a go at singing it. I promise you, you will feel better.

A prayer

Lord, thank you for the countryside, for our garden, for the flowers I have in my room. Lord, open my eyes to glory wherever it may be found.

Out in the open

Lord, how various are your works: in wisdom you have made them all and the earth is full of your creatures. There is the wide immeasurable sea: there move living things without number great and small. There go the ships to and fro: and there is that Leviathan whom you formed to sport in the deep.

The inspiration for this Psalm came out in the open. It must have done. My guess is that the writer had climbed up to a hill overlooking the sea. It was strikingly blue, all the more so because it was whipped up into little white waves by the steady breeze, enough to propel the sailing ships. And what was that sudden spurt of water like a fountain in the midst of the sea? Oh that? A whale! The deep sea is full of strange creatures, great and small. God's works are both many and various. All this you will only appreciate if you go outside into the open spaces and see what is to be seen there (not that we have any whales in Surrey, where I live!)

This Psalm advocates what might be called 'fresh-air religion'. It means going out into the world of nature and seeing God's handiwork there. This form of religion broadens the mind, sharpens the powers of observation and quickens the intellect. Let us not forget that God made his world for our welfare. We shall not be whole and wholesome if we shut ourselves up indoors all our time—no, not even for praying! We must learn to pray outside in the open.

I dare to say this although I now live in this lovely part of Surrey because almost the whole of my ministry has been spent in central London. For twenty years my study needed the electric light switched on even at the height of summer; but I found a park nearby where I walked for twenty minutes before breakfast. There was a pond there and the ducks on it found a place in my prayers. No, not as spectacular as what the Psalmist saw, but enough for thanksgiving.

A prayer

Lord, thank you for all lovely things in nature and for funny things; and if there have to be spiders as well, you know best.

The gracious creator

As for me, I will be talking of thy worship: thy glory, thy praise, and wondrous works; So that men shall speak of the might of thy marvellous acts: and I will also tell of thy greatness. The memorial of thin abundant kindness will be shewed: and men shall sing of thy righteousness. The Lord is gracious, and merciful: long-suffering, and of great goodness. The Lord is loving unto every man: and his mercy is over all his works. All thy works shall praise thee, O Lord: and thy saints give thanks unto thee.

As I write a robin is singing his little song on the silver birch tree outside my study window. Dusk is falling, so maybe he has had his supper and will soon be flitting off to roost. Nature has many vast scenes of panoramic splendour but many little touches of beauty as well. God's world is not a mere utility machine, nor simply functional. It is a delight. Have you seen the Andrex advertisement which portrays a woolly puppy with his paws crossed and looking so serious? Isn't it adorable? And there are not only beautiful things in the world but comic things to do us good. I was nearly doubled up with laughter in last week by a photograph in the newspaper of a man trying to mount the left side of a horse with his right foot in the stirrup! Picture the result!

Am I being trite? But 'All thy works shall praise thee, O Lord: and thy saints give thanks unto thee.' And if tomorrow someone sees you making your way to church, they could say, 'Fancy that! this man/woman must believe in God the creator!' That walk will be your visible witness and you will be fulfilling the first verse of today's reading.

Prayer

Lord, thank you for things to admire, things at which to laugh, and all the riches of nature, and for people to love: 'We praise thee, O God. We acknowledge thee to be the Lord.'

Power and glory

All thy works praise thee, O Lord: and thy saints give thanks unto thee. They shew the glory of thy kingdom: and talk of thy power; That thy power, thy glory, and mightiness of thy kingdom: might be known unto men.

In the autumn of 1987 a fierce storm swept across South-East England. It uprooted trees, blew down fences, stripped the tiles off countless roofs. It played havoc in my garden, taking nearly a year to put straight. Of course the devastation dominated the news for weeks. I can imagine however that in some parts of the world, perhaps where some of the readers of these notes live, a smile was raised at all the fuss we made. They live in the proximity of typhoons, whirlwinds, flooding on a massive scale, earth tremors and maybe even a volcanic eruption. What these people know, and what perhaps needed to be brought home to us, is the immense power in nature. It is irresistible by man.

But there is another aspect of nature besides power. There is glory. Even a frightening volcano in eruption is a sight to behold. And no matter what devastation is caused by the storms of nature, before long new growth takes over, with fresh green and flowers. Even some rocks are not left bare for ever, lichen covers them. If God is the Creator of all this, what can we learn about him?

The power of God is not naked. It is not without purpose. It is not wanton. Its aim is not destructive. The power of God is always linked to glory. This is why we can put away our fears of the future, our fear of death and what lies beyond death. We are destined for glory, and God has the power to bring about his glorious future.

A prayer

Wind and storm
Sunshine and flowers
All tell of you.
Help me to learn this lesson
and trust you with my future.

God's word in nature

He sendeth forth his commandment upon earth: and his word runneth very swiftly. He giveth snow like wool: and scattereth the hoar-frost like ashes. He casteth forth his ice like morsels: who is able to abide his frost? He sendeth out his word, and melteth them: he bloweth with his wind, and waters flow. He sheweth his word unto Jacob: his statutes and ordinances unto Israel. He hath not dealt so with any nation: neither have the heathen knowledge of his laws.

Those of us who have been brought up in the Christian tradition tend to think almost exclusively of the gospel in terms of redemption. This is a mistake. The good news, the gospel, is a twofold message—about the God who is Creator as well as Redeemer. Because the created order is his, it tells us about himself. The Bible, especially the Psalms, tell us that there is a word of God in nature because it is his. That's what it says at the start of today's reading: 'He sendeth forth his commandment upon earth: and his word runneth very swiftly.' There are lessons to be learnt about God from the flowers that bloom every spring; from the trees heavy with fruit just before the bareness of winter takes over; and from the sharp frosts killing off the insects before the new growth appears. The Psalmist was sensitive to all this. 'He giveth snow like wool: and scattereth the hoar-frost like ashes.'

I have had my eyes opened to all this now that I live in the country instead of central London. I shall never forget my first May here. The green and the blossom were breath-taking. This wonder tells us something about the wonder of God and his wondrous provision for us on this earth.

God through Christ has redeemed what he has made. But don't miss the word of God the Creator in nature because of the wonderful redemption of God the Saviour.

A prayer

For the beauty of the earth and for the beauty of the skies, I lift up my heart to you in thankfulness and praise—for you have created it, and you have given it.

The earth is the Lord's

Praise the Lord, O Jerusalem: praise thy God, O Sion. For he hath made fast the bars of thy gates: and hath blessed thy children within thee. He maketh peace in thy borders: and filleth thee with the flour of wheat. He sendeth forth his commandment upon earth: and his word runneth very swiftly. He giveth snow like wool: and scattereth the hoar-frost like ashes . . . He sendeth out his word, and melteth them: he bloweth with his wind, and the waters flow. He sheweth his word unto Jacob: his statutes and ordinances unto Israel. He hath not dealt so with any nation: neither have the heathen knowledge of his laws.

'The earth is the Lord's and they that dwell therein' (Psalm 24:1). His eye is upon them all for good, and there is a special providence for those who publicly acknowledge him as their sovereign Lord, here labelled as Jerusalem. Jews and Israel; for which we might read 'the Church' if we mean by it the whole company of God's faithful people.

God is concerned for our peace and safety—'for he hath made fast the bars of thy gates'—and for our sustenance, and not with rough barley bread but with 'the flour of wheat'. He is Lord of the forces of nature: frost and ice, wind and flowing waters, all operate at his will (commandment). It is *God's world* in which we live, not ours, and we ought to thank God that it has been given to us and recognize this, for therein is safety, our safety; God sees about it.

Idol-worshippers are in a different case–and the idols may not be visible, or tangible, but concepts of this world or its nations that have no place for God. Are the earth's resources safe in their hands?

A prayer

The earth is the Lord's and all that is therein: Let the congregation of saints praise him.

God's creation

Praise the Lord from the earth, you sea monsters and all deeps, fire and hail, snow and frost, stormy wind fulfilling his command! Mountains and all hills, fruit trees and all cedars! Beasts and all cattle, creeping things and flying birds!

The Prayer Book version of that last verse reads 'worms and feathered fowls'. When I was a choirboy I used to wonder how worms could praise the Lord. They wouldn't be invited to join *our* choir! I hope I have a little more perception now than at the age of seven and see that God's creation praises God when it performs the function for which it was created. Worms perform a necessary function in the garden. Burrowing around below the surface, as they do, they aerate the soil. They are praising God by doing that.

One Friday morning some three weeks ago I paid my weekly visit to our village baker's shop. On the way I passed a row of cottages. It was raining extremely hard and on the doorstep of one cottage, protected by a little roof, my attention was caught by a beautiful black cat. Now cats loathe getting wet, but this one was quite happy. It sat there, its tail curled around its feet. It was a picture of contentment and said in effect, 'The house is my home, I belong here, never mind the rain.' I thought to myself, 'For the people who live in that house, that cat must help to make it a home.'

A few days later I gave an old lady with two sticks a lift home from church in my car. It was raining. On the way she told me that she lived alone, and often days went by with no one to talk to. But she said, 'I have my cat, and I tell him everything. When he goes out to catch mice in the field next door he brings them in and lays them one by one at my feet. I always tell him he has done well! He likes it.'

Had God lonely people in mind when he made cats? Does he care for cats? Of course he does—and they praise God when they perform the function for which they were made. They catch mice, and praise him even more when they show in their funny feline fashion their appreciation of those who give them shelter.

A prayer

Lord, I praise you today, with your whole creation, for all the wonders of nature that surround us.

A new song

Praise the Lord! Sing to the Lord a new song, his praise in the assembly of the faithful! Let Israel be glad in his Maker, let the sons of Zion rejoice in their King! Let them praise his name with dancing, making melody to him with timbrel and lyre! For the Lord takes pleasure in his people; he adorns the humble with victory. Let the faithful exult in glory; let them sing for joy on their couches. Let the high praises of God be in their throats and two-edged swords in their hands, to wreak vengeance on the nations and chastisement on the peoples, to bind their kings with chains and their nobles with fetters of iron, to execute on them the judgment written! This is glory for all his faithful ones. Praise the Lord!

We can sing this Psalm quite merrily to start with. But then all of a sudden we stop. We can't sing the rest as Christians, can we? But I have included these verses in order to be honest. You would distrust me as a commentator if I kept only to the attractive bits. I am not going to explain these verses away. After the restoration of Israel in the time of Ezra and Nehemiah, when this Psalm was probably written, the nation *did* want to hit back at those who had hit them. We know that this is not in accordance with the Spirit of Christ. But some Christians have not been open about this. Using these very verses the Thirty Years War was started, a terrible bloody conflict in Germany. And Thomas Munzer appealed to the same verses when he stirred up the Peasants' War.

There now. I have got that off my chest. So the new song. What was it? The old song was the one they had been singing for ages to commemorate the deliverance from Egypt. But now there was a new deliverance to celebrate. Is this not so with us? We have had great deliverances in our lives in the past. But what about last week, or even yesterday? Haven't we a new song to sing of God's goodness to us?

A prayer

Lord, you have led me through many rough places. Here's my new song.

A reminder of glory

Praise the Lord. O praise God in his sanctuary: praise him in the firmament of his power. Praise him for his mighty acts: praise him according to his abundant goodness. Praise him in the blast of the ram's horn: praise him upon the lute and harp. Praise him with the timbrel and dances: praise him upon the strings and pipe. Praise him on the high sounding cymbals: praise him upon the loud cymbals. Let everything that has breath praise the Lord: O praise—the Lord.

This is how the Psalter ends, with a great burst of praise, every instrument brought in to swell the orchestra. This is the reaction that ought to summarize our faith, our prayers and all that we attempt in response to God's word and commandment. Praise the Lord! Or in Hebrew, *Hallelujah!*

Some forms of Christian worship are not as strong in praise as they ought to be. The very buildings are drab, the singing lifeless, the reading of the scriptures dull. But worship in whatever place should present in some form the element of glory. We have a glorious God, a glorious gospel, and we are destined for glory beyond the grave. It is for those responsible for worship to give us a glimpse of glory now. Perhaps no Christian church has understood this as well as the Orthodox Church, all the more significant because for so long it has had to bear its witness under conditions of oppression. The critic who in the midst of hardship sees only the gorgeous vestments and the priceless icons has missed the point. These things are a confession of faith, they remind of a glory to come. So does Psalm 150. 'Let everything that has breath praise the Lord.' What vigour! What faith! If only it were like that in all our churches.

Thanksgiving

When you first wake in the morning, unless you are one of those people who jump out of bed straightaway, you lie there for a few minutes thinking about the day ahead. Perhaps you do this with that early morning cup of tea. May I give you a little piece of advice? Don't run over the day's duties. Don't begin to face the pressing problems that will probably come your way. Start the day with the words 'Thank you' on your lips. For many people those words will express appreciation for being alive, perhaps alive and *well*. This is elementary but it is the way to start the day—with thanksgiving.

Thanksgiving for what? For food and shelter: it is very easy to take these basics for granted. For friends, if not for family, for some of its members may have died, but we can thank God for the memory of them. And then thanksgiving that we have a job to do, and sufficient health and strength to set about it. And thanksgiving for people we know who have come through their illnesses, trials and tribulations, thanksgiving, that is, for their deliverances. And thanksgiving for our faith. Remember we did not make it, it came to us, it was, and is, a gift from God. And there are other joys: the beauties of nature, the song of the birds, the magnificence of the starlit heavens at night.

Does all this mean taking time before getting going each day? Not really, we simply run the things over in our minds without articulating them. Two minutes then? Five minutes? But *to begin each day* in the right state of mind is the secret of a successful passage through life. The Psalmist understood this. There are more Psalms of thanksgiving than any other. Now read them, and you will be astonished at the variety.

Prayer

Lord, I take so much for granted. Make me a more thankful person, a more grateful person, a more sensitive person for what others do for me. Give me the grace to express my thanks and not to be churlish or offhand not only for big things, but also for little things. If we fail in the small, almost commonplace, matters, we shall fail in the big things. We shall fail to thank God for his wonderful creation, for his redemption bought at a price for us, and for his longsuffering when we slip back. A thankful person is a happy person, and a happy person is a benediction to a community. Lord, make me a happy Christian.

A merciful deliverance

O Lord, how many are my foes! Many are rising against me; many are saying of me, there is no help for him in God. But thou, O Lord, art a shield about me, my glory, and the lifter of my head. I cry aloud to the Lord, and he answers me from his holy hill. I like down and sleep; I wake again, for the Lord sustains me. I am not afraid of ten thousands of people who have set themselves against me round about.

Rub your eyes! Was there ever a more dismal sight—or an unbelievable sight? King David surrounded by his court taking to their heels because Absalom, the king's son of all people, was springing a *coup d'état*. How humiliating! How dangerous! And traitors in his own circle mocking his melancholy procession as it wound its anxious way out of Jerusalem heading for exile beyond the Jordan river and with no time to lose. Would they reach safety by nightfall? They did; otherwise they would have been decimated by Absalom's rebel army, and he, the king, led back in chains to his capital, the prisoner of his own son!

And when the sun rose next morning David prayed. What did he pray? Read the verse of Psalm 3 again, preferably out loud.

Have you ever been beaten down? But by the mercy of God you escaped calamity. Did words like this prayer of David escape your lips then? Yes, you really prayed then; so did I. We really did.

A prayer

Lord, but for your mercy where would I be today?

Thanks for God's mercies

I love thee, O Lord, my strength. The Lord is my rock, and my fortress, and my deliverer, my God, my rock, in whom I take refuge, my shield, and the horn of my salvation, my stronghold. I shall call upon the Lord, who is worthy to be praised, and I am saved from my enemies. The cords of death encompassed me, the torrents of perdition assailed me; the cords of Sheol entangled me, the snares of death confronted me.

The authorship of the various Psalms is not easy to determine. They are popularly called the Psalms of David but which of them he wrote is uncertain. The Psalm for our reading today however is the exception. This really is David's Psalm, or song, addressed to God on the day when God delivered him from the hand of all his enemies and from the hand of Saul. So says the brief historical note which prefaces the Psalm. Moreover the Psalm is set out in full in 2 Samuel 22 with this preface.

So here we see David breasting the tape at the close of his long marathon. The conflict with Saul dragged on and on, the fortunes of war were swaying backwards and forwards, its final outcome frequently in doubt. But David hung on, confident of his own uprightness and confident of God. And when at last he won through there was no boasting on his part, no clamouring for revenge, but sheer gratitude to God for seeing him through. There were times of deep darkness—'the cords of death encompassed me, the torrents of perdition assailed me'—but God gave him the victory.

If you are a young person reading this Psalm today you should recall some specific incident in your past (short as it may be) when you came out safely from a struggle. Perhaps an examination or the wearisome task of finding a job. Remember it vividly and then thank God for the happy outcome. Or if you are elderly (like me, the writer) you can look back over a long life with its mixture of the rough and the smooth, but remembering special times of deliverance. You didn't 'go under', you came through. Did you, did I, sing a song then like David in this Psalm? Well, sing it today. I will sing it. (Good thing you can't hear me!) But God has been my *refuge*, and my deliverer. To react to the past like this is the way to succeed in the future.

A prayer

Praise the Lord, O my soul, and bless his holy name. Time and time again you have delivered me when I could so easily have fallen. But you upheld me. Hallelujah.

Giving thanks

He brought me forth into a broad place; he delivered me, because he delighted in me. The Lord rewarded me according to my righteousness, according the cleanness of my hands he recompensed me. For I have kept the ways of the Lord, and have not wickedly departed from my God. For all his ordinances were before me, and his statutes I did not put away from me. I was blameless before him, and I kept myself from guilt. Therefore the Lord has recompensed me according to my righteousness, according to the cleanness of my hands in his sight.

This Psalm—Psalm 18—is to be found in 2 Samuel 22 under the heading 'And David spake unto the Lord the words of this song in the day that the Lord delivered him out of the hand of all his enemies and out of the hand of Saul.' So peace at last for David; no more an armed refugee on the roads, no more fear of terror behind every rock, every stunted shrub. David breathed again. But how did he celebrate his deliverance? A triumphal procession? An orgy of feasting and dancing? On the contrary, he lifted up his heart in thanksgiving to God first, whatever festivities might follow. He acknowledged that God was his deliverer, not simply his own military skill (which of course played its part), nor luck, nor fate, but God's mercies. Nor was he wrong to boast that he had not wickedly forsaken God. After all he hadn't killed Saul, the Lord's Anointed, when the chance was there. David had kept his hands tolerably clean.

The reality of our faith is shown by our actions when peace and prosperity come.

Prayer

Lord, it is not by my own skill only that I am. Praise be to your Name.

God's earth

The earth is the Lord's and the fullness thereof, the world and those who dwell therein; for he has founded it upon the seas, and established it upon the rivers.

A few days ago I met a lady who said she was very sad. I braced myself wondering if perhaps she had lost some member of the family. But no, she was sad because her gander whom she had looked after and loved for nearly nine years had died. I trod carefully because 'townee' that I am really, I wasn't sure I knew what a gander was. Of course I ought to have remembered the nursery rhyme 'Goosey goosey gander' but my nursery days are a long way back now. A gander is a male goose and this lady loved hers. It was part of her life.

I haven't any animals to look after myself but I can see how much they contribute to people's happiness. And I believe God meant it to be like this. If you read the story of the creation in Genesis you will notice the order of events there. First light separated from darkness, then living space, then vegetation, then living creatures which includes birds and animals (ganders too!), and then, not till all was ready, were man and woman created. Thus all was set for their welfare and pleasure. So the words of our Psalm, 'The earth is the Lord's and the fullness thereof.' So the text in 1 Timothy 6:17 'God . . . giveth us richly all things to enjoy.' I know we can abuse God's creation, we can be cruel to animals, we can turn the countryside into a desert—that is another matter and it is

wicked—what I want to emphasize today is not that but rejoicing for all the good things God has given us.

Christians should not have their eyes closed to beauty, they should not be unresponsive to the lovely things there are in the world, they should be ready to laugh at funny things and sing when possible and certainly listen to singing. Christians should not be narrow, tight-lipped and loveless. Christians must be open—to people, to God's world (he made it): 'The earth is the Lord's and the fullness thereof.'

The other day I was told of a dog which had to be taken to the vet for a nasty operation on his back requiring an anaesthetic. He obviously disliked it intensely but as soon as he 'came round', up on his feet again he walked to where he knew his lead had been placed, picked it up in his mouth and went to his mistress, saying in effect, 'I'm ready now, let's go and enjoy ourselves.' Is there a lesson for us here?

Prayer

Lord, make me a happy person, happy in myself, happy so as to make others happy who come across my path through the faith we have in the risen Christ.

Communal thanks

I will bless the Lord at all times; his praise shall continually be in my mouth. My soul makes its boast in the Lord; let the afflicted hear and be glad. O magnify the Lord with me, and let us exalt his name together!

When I read these verses I am reminded of the parable Jesus told of the man who lost one of his hundred sheep. When he found it he didn't just sit down with a sigh of relief. Oh no! He called his friends and neighbours together crying, 'Rejoice with me! I have found my lost sheep!' And when a woman lost one of her ten precious silver pieces and then found it she didn't simply carry on with her domestic duties with a light heart. She called her friends and neighbours together saying, 'Rejoice with me! I have found the piece that I lost!' And when the prodigal son returned home, his father laid on the biggest party the house had ever seen. Not one of these three—a shepherd, a housewife and a father—believed they could rejoice as they felt the urge to rejoice, *unless* they found people to rejoice with them.

So this is the point: we can't properly praise God in isolation. Of course we thank God, I hope, in our private prayer for the many good things he gives us. Every day before I get dressed I say out loud, and sometimes even sing, the first two verses of the *Te Deum*; but this isn't enough. From time to time we have to join with other people who are praising; this means the congregation of Christian people, perhaps in church. And this is one of the Church's great provisions—a place and a company of men, women and children where praising, rejoicing, singing and thanksgiving are regularly carried out. So when you and I have something to sing about, and such times are not that rare (even today's world isn't all gloom), we mustn't keep it all to ourselves. We must make our way to the local church, or wherever there is a Christian gathering, and sing for all we are worth. Read Psalm 34 again. 'O magnify the Lord with me, and let us exalt his name together!' And know this. A congregation heartily singing is uplifting for the individual. And if you live alone, and I know that some of you do, don't miss out on the congregational worship.

A prayer

Lord, I thank you for many blessings—and I thank you that in your love you have given me friends to sing your praises with me.

Rescue

I waited patiently for the Lord; he inclined to me and heard my cry. He drew me up from the desolate pit, out of the miry bog, and set my feet upon a rock, making my steps secure. He put a new song in my mouth, a song of praise to our God. Many will see and fear, and put their trust in the Lord.

You will be wasting your time reading these Psalms if your religion is mostly theory. In these Psalms we come alongside people, perhaps David was one of them, who tasted life in all its bittersweetness and found God there. Some of them, like the writer of this Psalm 40, went down into a miry bog with no sure foothold, no not literally, but the bog of uncertainty how to go on living.

This could be brought about by a bereavement. The rooms in the house feel horribly empty, painfully silent, there seems no point in planning anything, all the days are the same. Or the bog of uncertainty could be brought about by a disfigurement, or by a crushing sense of incompetence in comparison with others in our circle, or it could be plain shortage of money crippling our way of life, or the loss of love on the part of someone close to us, perhaps threatening or even leading to marriage breakdown. Loneliness is a frightening miry pit with no rock on which to gain a firm foothold.

But the Psalmist cried to God for help, he waited patiently for God to come to his rescue. No, let us be realistic. Not even God can reverse all adverse circumstances. If a man in hospital has had a leg amputated God cannot give him a new one. And bereavement has to be 'gone through', it cannot be reversed. There is however an instrument sufficient to enable us to 'go on' or to 'overcome' as St John in his Epistle puts it (1 John 5:4). It is faith. We can *believe* that God has not forgotten us in that miry bog, he has his hand on our life still and in due time we shall be pulled out, perhaps in a surprising fashion. Then perhaps verse 3 of our reading today will happen.

Prayer

Lord, give us grace to wait patiently for you and one day, if not today, to sing.

Three basics

I waited patiently for the Lord: and he inclined to me and heard my cry. He brought me up from the pit of roaring waters out of the mire and clay: and set my feet upon a rock and made firm my foothold. And he has put a new song in my mouth: even a song of thanksgiving to our God. Many shall see it and fear: and shall put their trust in the Lord.

I really don't like verse 2. I prefer the Prayer Book version: 'He brought me also out of the horrible pit.' The Hebrew word for 'pit' here is *bor*, and it means not a well with fresh, bubbling or even roaring water, but a hole dug in the ground in which to store the winter rain water for the summer drought. It was in fact a cistern, and at the end of the summer it contained no water, only a slimy, muddy sludge. There were cisterns like this all over Palestine, and woe betide anyone who fell into one. It was a horrible pit.

Here in this Psalm is someone pulled up out of this predicament. Note three points—a desperate man's cry for help; a wonderful deliverance from disaster; a song of thanksgiving. May I suggest that none of us has a real religion without knowing some experiences of all three? Yes, the horrible pit would be some sink of iniquity into which we have fallen. More likely for most of us it might be a sense of inadequacy—'I just can't cope any more.' Or, 'The bottom is falling out of my life.' A marriage is breaking up, perhaps, or the threat of some devastating illness. 'O God, bring me up out of the pit where I am sinking.' Then sec-ondly the experience of deliverance. If our faith cannot do anything to pull us out of trouble, perhaps by assisting us through it, we have no real faith. The essence of the New Testament proclamation is that we have a Saviour who is Christ the Lord. And then thirdly, a song of thanksgiving. If we cannot sing *because of our faith*, we have seriously missed out.

The bride

The King's daughter is all glorious within: her clothing is of wrought gold. She shall be brought unto the King in raiment of needlework: the virgins that be her fellows shall bear her company, and shall be brought into thee. With joy and gladness shall they be brought: and shall enter into the King's palace. Instead of thy fathers thou shalt have children: whom thou mayest make princes in all lands. I will remember thy Name from one generation to another: therefore shall the people give thanks unto thee, world without end.

Now be honest. These verses might as well be left standing in their original Hebrew for all the impact they make on us setting out for a busy day at the office or grappling with some complicated family problem.

This Psalm is about a wedding. The earlier verses tell of the bridegroom, what a splendid man he is. Then we see him on the way to the bride's home to fetch her back to his own house. In today's reading we see the girl, the king's daughter, waiting within her home, beautifully dressed, and all the bridesmaids grouped around her. Isn't she lovely? Then they go off in procession to the bridegroom's house 'with joy and gladness'. What a day! And a promise of children to come. God is to be praised for such a happy event.

Whose marriage is this? King Jehoram of Israel and Athaliah of Judah? Possibly. But doesn't it all point away to Christ making the Church his bride? (See Ephesians 5:25–27.) Sometimes we might be tempted to ask, 'What on earth can he see in the Church that is attractive?' But he takes us as we are, and one day we shall be a glorious Church, without all those blemishes which are so distressing. So cheer up! Let these puzzling (at first anyway) verses do that for you.

Prayer

Yes, Lord, I will go on my way rejoicing.

Daily thanksgiving

It is good to give thanks to the Lord, to sing praises to thy name, O Most High; to declare thy steadfast love in the morning, and thy faithfulness by night, to the music of the lute and the harp, to the melody of the lyre. For thou, O Lord, hast made me glad by thy work; at the works of thy hands I sing for joy. How great are thy works, O Lord! Thy thoughts are very deep! The dull man cannot know, the stupid cannot understand this.

Yes, I did. I gave thanks to the Lord soon after I awoke this morning. I can't say I sang praises, and certainly there was no accompaniment of lute and harp. One of my deficiencies—I have many—is that I can't play any musical instrument—but I went over in my mind causes for thanksgiving. I try to do this at the beginning of each day. There is always something for which to praise God, though apparently quite small, trivial. And at night before I go to sleep I run over in my mind the good things that have happened, frequently most ordinary things, like the garden machinery mechanic who said he would call to collect my mower for servicing and he did! Our Psalm today says, 'It is good to give thanks to the Lord, to sing praises to thy name, O Most High.' And then this 'the dull man cannot know, the stupid cannot understand this'. We are far more likely to be well in body and mind if we give proper place to thanksgiving in our lives. Discontent and ingratitude pull us down.

A few weeks ago I nearly 'came a cropper' on this resolve to keep the good and lovely things in mind; I thought I would let the garden go a bit this year. And then my eye caught a little cluster of snowdrops blooming merrily outside my study window and I was rebuked. They were praising God in their way. And it will not be long after Easter before that blackbird starts filling the garden with his song as he does every spring (is it the same one?) even though he will find some of the branches in the silver birch tree lopped off where he usually perches. So I will make a point of making my garden as decorative as I can. God has given us good and lovely things and we praise God, the Creator, by caring for them and rejoicing in them, and are better people for doing so.

Prayer

Lord, I praise you for the good things you have given me—my garden, lovely flowers, the kindness of neighbours and the love of some particular people, but above all for the wonder of the Easter message of newness of life.

Thankfulness

O come, let us sing unto the Lord: let us heartily rejoice in the strength of our salvation. Let us come before his presence with thanksgiving: and shew ourselves glad in him with psalms. For the Lord is a great God: and a great King above all gods. In his hand are all the corners of the earth: and the strength of the hills is his also. The sea is his, and he made it: and his hands prepared the dry land. O come, let us worship and fall down: and kneel before the Lord our Maker.

On rising each morning, we should all ask ourselves one question, 'What have I to thank God for today?' Perhaps the rain is streaming down and we have planned a day in the country. Perhaps the car has broken down just when we needed it. Perhaps we are confined to bed with an illness. Perhaps we have failed our examinations. Perhaps a friend has let us down. We all know about frustrations.

Do we all know how important it is to look round, even on those dark days, for something for which to be thankful? Maybe only a little thing—never mind, fix on it. 'I can't see very well but my hearing is good.' People who make a point of thanksgiving are the ones who are not defeated by 'the changes and chances of this mortal life'.

Now read the Psalm again. It tells us what the ground of our thanksgiving can be. God is the Lord of all life, even ours. God has in his control the deep places of life (here translated 'corners') and the exhilarating mountain-top experiences as well. Even the sea is his, and the Hebrews hated the sea; they saw it as full of chaos and horrible monsters! So, as God is Lord of all, is it beyond us to find at least one thing today for which to be thankful?

A prayer

Lord, I thank you for this, and this and this; and for him and for her. Hear me now trying to sing.

Cheerfulness

O be joyful in the Lord, all ye lands: serve the Lord with gladness, and come before his presence with a song. Be ye sure that the Lord he is God: it is he that hath made us, and not we ourselves; we are his people, and the sheep of his pasture. O go your way into his gates with thanksgiving, and into his courts with praise: be thankful unto him, and speak good of his Name. For the Lord is gracious, his mercy is everlasting: and his truth endureth from generation to generation.

I ought to be cheerful today, 'serving the Lord with gladness and coming before his presence with a song'. The sun is shining, I feel reasonably well, and some of you have written me kind letters—I wish I could reply to them all. But I am a bit grumpy. Three years ago a friend gave us a lovely climbing rose called 'Golden Shower' to mark our wedding anniversary—and this summer for the very first time it produced a gorgeous crop of golden blooms. But this morning, there isn't a flower left. Squirrels have nibbled them all off. So that's why I am a bit grumpy.

But I know that I shouldn't be. After all, the loss of these flowers is not a major tragedy. But isn't this so often the way we let things spoil our life? A little mishap puts us right off our stroke and other people suffer because of it.

For some years, until leukaemia claimed her, a friend worked five days a week as my voluntary secretary. I never knew her to be anything else but consistently pleasant, and I put this down to her natural good manners. But I did her an injustice. One day she said to me, 'I think it is quite wrong to offload one's personal troubles on to other people.' I knew then that her consistent cheerfulness was the outcome of personal effort. She had decided to live Psalm 100—her *Jubilate*.

I wish I had remembered her and Psalm 100 when I saw my lovely roses this morning—destroyed by squirrels.

A prayer

Lord, it is so often the little mishaps that throw us. Teach me not to spoil other people's lives by my thoughtlessness.

Past deliverances

O give thanks unto the Lord, and call upon his Name: tell the people what things he hath done. O let your songs be of him, and praise him: and let your talking be of all his wondrous works. Rejoice in his holy Name: let the heart of them rejoice that seek the Lord. Seek the Lord and his strength: seek his face evermore. Remember the marvellous works that he hath done: his wonders, and the judgements of his mouth.

I have just been reading an extract from a German book with the alarming title of *Flight into Hell*. It told of a pilot flying solo who had to make an emergency landing in the deserted outback of Australia, and in particular of one night. He had come to 'the end of himself' on account of hunger and thirst and utter loneliness, almost to the point of craziness. All the strength of his young manhood was gone. And then, in that night (would he ever forget it?) he grasped at the faith that there is a power beyond our power and stronger than ours; in prayer he laid hold of it. He lived to tell the tale, giving it this startling title.

Perhaps you can recount from your own experience some such breath-taking occasion. I cannot, but I remember, when I was a very little boy, seeing the house almost opposite ours a ruin from a shell fired from a German battleship in the First World War. The shell failed to explode. We suffered no damage. My life, however, has been undramatic: perhaps yours has too. But do we *know* from what dangers and adversities we have been saved? As I look back I am aware, as once I was not, of some of the pitfalls into which I might have blundered and didn't.

The verses from today's Psalm are all about recalling with thanks and praise God's deliverances on our behalf. Read the last verse again. Have you not been ill and gone back to work again? Have you not lost something or someone, at some time, and wondered how you would ever manage? But you have. My friend! A song is due from you and I will join you in the chorus.

A prayer

Lord, I don't praise you enough, I don't thank you enough. Today I will search around in the past and look closely at the present till I sing a little, or whistle a little as best I can.

Forebears

Remember the marvellous works that he hath done: his wonders, and the judgements of his mouth, O ye seed of Abraham his servant: ye children of Jacob his chosen. He is the Lord our God: his judgements are in all the world. He hath been always mindful of his covenant and promise: that he made to a thousand generations; even the covenant that he made with Abraham: and the oath that we sware unto Isaac; And appointed the same unto Jacob for a law: and to Israel for an everlasting testament.

Looking down on me, to the left of my desk, is a portrait of my grandfather, not a religious man though a church-goer of sorts. He was devoted to helping the underprivileged and unfortunate in the city where he lived.

I wonder what I owe to him. I have no idea. Most of us never reckon with the possibility that we are partly what we are because of our forebears. We see ourselves as largely isolated individuals. This is not the view of the Bible. In our verses today from Psalm 105 Abraham is mentioned twice, and Isaac his son, and Jacob his grandson. Abraham set the standard for his family that came after, and for all the nation of Israel of which he was the forebear. Abraham was never forgotten. Thanks and praise were perpetually offered to God for what he had given through this man, imperfect though he was.

From our forebears we receive something of our particular disposition and attitude to life. Whatever measure of contentment and achievement we enjoy now is partly due to them; we cannot claim all the credit for ourselves. What

Israel as a nation became stemmed from Abraham's pioneering faith.

Have you some photographs in your home of your parents, grandparents, greatgrandparents? I would be surprised if you hadn't. Well, go and stand in front of them for a moment or two and thank God at the remembrance of them and what they have passed down to you.

A prayer

Lord, thank you for my father and mother and for my grandparents, and their grandparents; and for aunts and uncles, and my whole family circle— Thank you for what you have given me through them, and save me from forgetfulness.

God's enduring love

It is good to give thanks to the Lord, for his love endures for ever. So let them say who were redeemed by the Lord, redeemed by him from the power of the enemy and gathered out of every land, from east and west, from north and south.

This long Psalm (43 verses) is all about *cheseth*, a key word in the Old Testament. It means loving kindness. Perhaps 'love' is better, certainly less likely to be misunderstood than 'mercy', as in the Prayer Book version. All this about love, however, could sound rather vague and like pious 'clap-trap', but not in this Psalm! Four illustrations are provided, taken from life and experience, which we shall read in turn. Then there is a summary of God's actions and an application in these words: 'Let the wise men lay these things to heart, and ponder the record of the Lord's *cheseth* [enduring love]' (v. 43).

Note how this 'confession' of the reality of God's love is spoken by those with sharp experience of being redeemed. They have been brought back from the power of an enemy, in whatever form that may have taken. They have felt scattered, without any sense of belonging and without roots. This in a literal sense is the plight of refugees, of whom, sad to say, we have many examples in the modern world. It is, however, an all too common experience spiritually. In the midst of plenty there can be an emptiness of soul. Meaninglessness or pointlessness is the frequent outcome.

Some of us have not known how this feels. I am one of them. I was brought up in a Christian home. We went to church by the time we could toddle (I was a choirboy at seven!) Our danger, however, is that we shall take *cheseth*, God's enduring love, for granted. So in the next few days let us attend to Psalm 107, and next time you hear it sung, which I hope you will, you will feel more in tune with it!

A prayer

Lord, let me remember your enduring love today shown beyond compare in the death and resurrection of Christ for our salvation.

Gone astray

O give thanks unto the Lord, for he is gracious: and his mercy endureth for ever. Let them give thanks whom the Lord hath redeemed: and delivered from the hand of the enemy; And gathered them out of the lands, from the east, and from the west: from the north, and from the south. They went astray in the wilderness out of the way: and found no city to dwell in; Hungry and thirsty: their soul fainted in them. So they cried unto the Lord in their trouble: and he delivered them from their distress. He led them forth by the right way: that they might go to the city where they dwelt.

A week or two ago I overheard two women talking. It was a Sunday. They were obviously mothers with teenage children commiserating with each other. One said, 'I brought mine up to go to church regularly and they did for a time, but not now.' To which the other replied, 'Same with my family, they never think of going to church now.' Both the mothers apparently were regular church members.

We have a word for such young people. We call them 'lapsed Christians'. Sad to say, there are many such in the modern world. Sorely tempted by the excitements of our technological age, they simply write off the Church and all that it stands for as boring. They want sensation, and are prepared to employ artificial devices to heighten it. But what are the long term results? Contentment? A sense of meaning in life? Peace of mind? Happy relationships? Good physical and mental heath? The answers are obvious. Listen to this Psalm again, 'They went astray in the wilderness out

of the way: and found no city to dwell in.' Meaningless is the name of the foreign land where multitudes live today.

Some escape. They come back. They rediscover faith. The story of the prodigal son which Jesus told happens today. It may not be all that long before our churches fill up again with worshippers. Spiritual hunger is a reality. God gathers his people together in his own good time for his mercy 'endureth for ever'.

A prayer

Lord, remember . . . and . . . who have given up church-going and the Christian way of life. Bring them back, Lord, to the right way.

Losing the way

Some lost their way in desert wastes; they found no road to a city to live in; hungry and thirsty, their spirit sank within them. So they cried to the Lord in their trouble, and he rescued them from their distress; he led them by a straight and easy way until they came to a city to live in. Let them thank the Lord for his enduring love and for the marvellous things he has done for men: he has satisfied the thirsty and filled the hungry with good things.

I was driving the car out west from the centre of London by a main road I knew like the back of my hand. After a mile or more I came to a fork in the road and took the left fork when I should have gone straight on. I drove for three or four miles till I realized that I did not know where I was. I did not recognize any of the buildings. At last I pulled up and reversed. There was nothing for it but to return to the fork where I supposed I had taken the wrong turning. This took time and made me late. I was cross with myself. All the same, I had a sense of relief that I knew now where I was. I am not sure whether I thanked the Lord for his enduring love that I had rediscovered the right way, but I might have done.

Can it be that our whole community has taken the wrong turning and now we have lost our way? By and large church-going has been abandoned and standards of morality are counted as 'fuddy-duddy'. Freedom is the 'in thing'. Everyone must do as he or she thinks right. We see a startling increase in the break-up of family life and in marriages drifting after a year or two on to the rocks. We see nervous breakdowns and suicide. We should go back to the right road, and God would be gracious. Difficulties and hardships will always turn up but there will also be an inner sense of satisfaction. We shall enjoy life's journey again.

A prayer

Lord, give us the wisdom
not simply to push on
when it is obvious
that we have taken the wrong road.

The empty soul

O that men would therefore praise the Lord for his goodness: and declare the wonders that he doeth for the children of men! For he satisfieth the empty soul: and filleth the hungry soul with goodness. Such as sit in darkness, and in the shadow of death: being fast bound in misery and iron; Because they rebelled against the words of the Lord: and lightly regarded the counsel of the most Highest; He also brought down their heart through heaviness: they fell down and there was none to help them. So when they cried unto the Lord in their trouble: he delivered them out of their distress. For he brought them out of darkness, and out of the shadow of death: and brake their bonds in surrender.

I wonder if you have ever said sadly of someone you know, 'I am afraid there isn't much in him (or in her)'. I was reading the other day about a young man who produced just that reaction in me. His life-style had consisted of fast motor cars, late night parties, the most up-to-date fashions in food and drink and an apparently endless series of girlfriends. Altogether an empty life. And it all indicated an empty soul. There was a photograph of him at that stage in his life and I could read it in his face. The eyes and the mouth told of utter boredom. It is not difficult to understand how such poor people (and they are poor, though well supplied with money) can commit suicide. Meaninglessness kills them.

But them something happened to this young man. He became a caring, diligent family man. People were surprised. The man with 'nothing in him' began to exhibit sheer goodness. It all happened after he experienced a personal loss that really hurt. The distress came first. Then the deliverance.

Now read today's verses again. Don't they begin to take on new meaning?

Sad to say there are crowds of empty people in our modern world. Some have never known what it is to have to 'go without'. Contentment does not come that way. Maybe some form of hardship will have to be experienced before they will know it. Today's Psalm tells us that God satisfies the empty soul. What a wonder! What a promise!

A prayer

Lord, I pray for . . . and for . . . for those who do not seem to have found any real satisfaction in life.

Hooked

Some sat in darkness, dark as death, prisoners bound fast in iron, because they had rebelled against God's commands and flouted the purpose of the Most High. Their spirit was subdued by hard labour; they stumbled and fell with none to help them. So they cried to the Lord in their trouble, and he saved them from their distress; he brought them out of darkness, dark as death, and broke their chains. Let them thank the Lord for his enduring love and for the marvellous things he has done for men: he has shattered doors of bronze, bars of iron he has snapped in two.

I have no experience of what it is like to be hooked on drugs. That is to say, I have never actually encountered anyone in that condition. But I have read about it. The most frightening aspect is the destruction it causes of the entire personality. A man or woman truly hooked on drugs is practically useless either to himself or herself, or to anyone else. And the outcome all too frequently is crime.

I mention drug addiction because it is one form in which 'sitting in darkness, dark as death, prisoners bound fast in iron' takes place in the modern world. We ought not to write off the Psalm as having reference only to the captivity of Israel in the sixth century BC. And people do not only get hooked on drugs, but on drink, gambling and sexual licence. They get dragged down to a place where they cannot do without these narcotics. Some in clinics and other institutions are set free. Some, no doubt, cry to God in their distress. It is interesting that when life turns sour people remember prayer. Very often it is a last resort. The wonder is that even so God is willing to hear.

They should thank the Lord for his enduring love. So should we all. Let us remember that God's will is that we should be free, not hooked on anything.

A prayer

Lord who came to set at liberty those who are captive, strengthen and support all who work for the liberation of men and women today from the bondage of alcoholism, drug addiction, sexual anarchy, and all that drags them down.

Suffering fools

Some were fools, they took to rebellious ways, and for their transgression they suffered punishment. They sickened at the sight of food and drew near to the very gates of death. So they cried to the Lord in their trouble, and he saved them from their distress; he sent his word to heal them and bring them alive out of the pit of death. Let them thank the Lord for his enduring love and for the marvellous things he has done for men. Let them offer sacrifices of thanksgiving and recite his deeds with shouts of joy.

I know it is quite wrong of me, and I admit it, but I do find it difficult to suffer fools gladly. When people abuse their own bodies on which they depend for the enjoyment of life—and life is meant to be enjoyed—so abuse them that they sicken at the sight of food, perhaps draw near to the very gate of death, I want to say, 'Well, it serves you right, doesn't it? You shouldn't have been such a fool', and leave the matter there.

But suppose the man or woman says, 'Yes, I have been a fool . . .' I ought to have been compassionate before, but I ought to be more than compassionate if the person owns up. I am expressing this personally for I am sure you are far more commendable in your attitude to fools than I am. I don't want to sound as if I am talking down to you, my patient readers!

Jesus was not, however, weak about fools. The man who thought he need bother no more was called a fool and so were the five girls who took no extra oil in case their lamps went out. Our Lord expects us to live and act as responsible beings and to think. But we have to remember that there are people whose personalities have been damaged through no fault of their own. Jesus said that it was the sick who needed a physician, not those who were well.

A prayer

*Knock down my pride, Lord
and keep it knocked down.
I haven't anything
you didn't give me,
even the ability to read this.*

Waves and storms

Others there are who go to sea in ships and make their living on the wide waters. These men have seen the acts of the Lord and his marvellous doings in the deep. At his command the storm-wind rose and lifted the waves high. Carried up to heaven, plunged down to the depths, tossed to and fro in peril, they reeled and staggered like drunken men, and their seamanship was all in vain. So they cried to the Lord in their trouble, and he brought them out of their distress . . . Let them thank the Lord for his enduring love and for the marvellous things he has done for men.

I have a little laugh all to myself when I read these verses and note the sequence. First people who have lost their way, then people who are enslaved, followed by people who are fools. The next calamity is people who go to sea in ships! I am sure the Psalmist did not mean to be funny, for I know the Hebrews hated the sea. Nevertheless, some of them 'went to sea in ships' and made 'their living on the wide waters'. And of course they had frightening experiences. They were 'tossed to and fro in peril'. And when I think of people sailing solo round the world and negotiating Cape Horn, as was done not so very long ago, I stand aghast. I can understand why it is sometimes said, 'You can't be a sailor and not believe in God.' It is the calm and the storms, the storms and the calm, that drive sailors to think about God, not least when safely back in port.

Life is like a voyage across a sea which is sometimes lovely and at other times frightening. We seem so small then, in the hands of forces beyond our control. What we have to remember is that even those forces are in the hands of God. Whatever happens we cannot fall out of the hands of God.

A prayer

Lord, I have been through some rough patches in life.
I have enjoyed some wonderful stretches, too.
In the rough and the smooth (and who knows what tomorrow will bring),
let me trust you.

The secret of happiness

He turns a desert into pools of water, a parched land into springs of water. And there he lets the hungry dwell, and they establish a city to live in; they sow fields, and plant vineyards, and get a fruitful yield.

There come in the lives of most of us patches which are like a desert, we 'write them off' as wastelands, nothing good will come of them. But we may be wrong. Sometimes those are the productive periods. This is what today's verses from Psalm 107 are all about. God turns a desert into pools of water and then there is growth, even a harvest.

Here is a story. It comes from the pen of a man called Harold Eeman, a Belgian, caught up in the First World War and who later entered the Belgian diplomatic service.

Describing his experience in the prisoner-of-war camp, he wrote, 'As I sat on the ground with unseeing eyes on the grey landscape, my loneliness overwhelmed me like a tidal wave. I plumbed hitherto unknown depths of human misery.' It was an experience that was never to recur. Nor would it ever be forgotten! Then he was moved to the notorious camp at Cassel known among the prisoners as Death Camp on account of the typhus epidemic. Then in 1917 British prisoners of war began to arrive and he offered to help attend the wounded though knowing little of medical skills, but this is what he wrote:

'The hours that left such nightmarish memories were the prelude to what strangely proved to be the happiest period of my prison life. To the days that followed, days of anxiety and exhausting work I owe the blessing of learning in my early twenties one of the greatest lessons that life can teach, a truth so many fail to discover, that happiness is not to be won by self-seeking but lies in forgetting oneself to seek the happiness of others.'

Prayer

Lord, teach me this secret of happiness.

Thank God

I love the Lord because he heard my voice: the voice of my supplication; because he inclined his ear to me: in the day that I called to him. The cords of death encompassed me the snares of the grave took hold of me: I was in anguish and sorrow. Then I called upon the name of the Lord: 'O Lord, I beseech you, deliver me!' Gracious and righteous is the Lord: full of compassion is our God. The Lord preserves the simple: when I was brought low he saved me.

Here is a man tossing and turning on his sick-bed. His temperature is raging, his throat scorches, his limbs ache. He crumples up with the pain. His doctors and nurses do all they can to ease his agony, but with next to no avail. Then at last, between his gasps, he manages an appeal to God. There seems to be no other help.

The learned commentaries tell us that this Psalm formed part of the Great Hallel, the great hymn of praise made up of Psalms 113–118; and this particular Psalm, number 116, was sung in Jewish homes at Passover celebrations. But *originally* it derived from such a bed of sickness that the sufferer never expected to 'pull through'; but he did.

What action do you take when you have been pulled back from some dreadful calamity? Do you celebrate your deliverance? Throw a party perhaps? To whom do you express your thanks? The doctor, perhaps, or the nurses? Yes, you give them a present. And your wife/husband who has born so patiently with you. But what about God? For all the skill and compassion of those who cared for you, the issues of life and death lie in God's hands. And some of you have actually been brought back from the jaws of death. The author of this Psalm got it right.

Thanks and praise

I love the Lord because he heard my voice: the voice of my supplication; because he inclined his ear to me: in the day that I called to him. The cords of death encompassed me, the snares of the grave took hold on me: I was in anguish and sorrow. Then I called upon the name of the Lord: 'O Lord I beseech you deliver me!' . . . I will offer you a sacrifice of thanksgiving: and call upon the name of the Lord. I will pay my vows to the Lord: in the presence of all his people, in the courts of the house of the Lord: even in your midst O Jerusalem. Praise the Lord.

Here is a man tossing and turning on his bed. His fever won't let him rest. His head feels as if it is splitting and every bone in his body aches. He is almost delirious with pain. His doctors and nurses do all they can to ease his wretchedness but not very successfully. They wonder if he will pull through. He, poor man, doubts it. Desperate, he utters an anguished prayer to God. He does pull through. He feels his recovery is God's answer, and when he is sufficiently strong to manage the journey he goes to the house of God to offer him thanks and praise.

Perhaps you have never 'touched bottom' like this. I nearly wrote 'you are lucky', but I take that back. None of us *has* to know deliverance from death to be truly thankful. Some of us thank God every day of our lives for the good things that come our way. As I write, the autumn sunshine is streaming across my desk and the pink geraniums are still making quite a show in the garden. 'Praise the Lord, O my soul!' Yes, thanksgiving should lead into praise. It is a poor, crabbed existence that has not enough thanksgiving in it to lead us from time to time into the house of God to praise him. And if a recovery from illness, like the Psalmist's, has spurred us on, we ought to sing all the louder (if in tune all the better!)

A prayer

*Lord, listen to me singing
above the clatter of my lawn-mower
today.
I have so much for which to be thankful,
not least that I have some grass to mow.*

Out of the dark

The voice of joy and health is in the dwellings of the righteous: the right hand of the Lord bringeth mighty things to pass . . . I shall not die, but live: and declare the works of the Lord. The Lord hath chastened and corrected me: but he hath not given me over unto death. Open me the gates of righteousness: that I may go unto them, and give thanks unto the Lord. This is the gate of the Lord: the righteous shall enter into it. I will thank thee, for thou hast heard me: and art become my salvation.

This Psalm would suit Saturday morning. Saturday morning feels different from Monday morning. We ease up on Saturdays. So sit back. What sort of week has it been? Easy? Smooth? No problems? No pain? No one been a bit nasty to you? No upsets? No loneliness? This Psalm sits back (as it were) recalling rough experiences in the past. But all that is over now. The Lord has brought 'mighty things to pass', calamity did not after all win the day. Joy can ring out and health be enjoyed. Prayer has been answered. God has come to the rescue.

Actually this Psalm is a processional hymn belonging perhaps to Maccabean times. The temple, long in ruins, was now rebuilt. What a thrill! There was a grand opening day of thanksgiving. (The choir in procession sang verses 1–18 pausing at the entrance to sing verse 19, then those waiting to receive them there sang the following verses, all joining together in verse 29.) What a day! And this was the Psalm Jesus led his disciples in singing (part of what is called the Hallel) on the Thursday night when he went out to the Garden of Gethsemane and to be crucified. Can you believe it? You must.

Don't tell me you have no experience of coming out of dark tunnels in life. Then you hardly know what thanksgiving is.

Prayer

Lord you have brought me out of the dark, and one day I shall be ever in the light.

59

Marvellous in our eyes

Open to me the gates of righteousness, that I may enter through them and give thanks to the Lord. This is the gate of the Lord; the righteous shall enter through it. I thank thee that thou hast answered me and hast become my salvation. The stone which the builders rejected has become the head of the corner. This is the Lord's doing; it is marvellous in our eyes. This is the day which the Lord has made; let us rejoice and be glad in it.

Perhaps you are hurrying off to work or sitting in the commuter train, which you use for your 'quiet time before God' (and why not?). How can you be expected to give your mind to what happened at the rebuilding of the Jewish temple after the Jewish people returned from that devastating defeat in war, all centuries before Christ? Perhaps, though, if I tell you a little you will experience something like turning on a light in a dark cupboard. Today's verses sound all right, but what do they mean? Let me tell you.

The great precession of priests and people had just reached the gates of the newly restored temple. 'Open to me the gates of righteousness,' cried the leader, 'that I may enter through them and give thanks to the Lord.' And those waiting to receive them called out 'This is the gate of the Lord, the righteous shall enter through it.' And then, looking up, they marvelled to see the rebuilt and restored temple—built of the very same stones that had lain around in ruins for years, stones which they had thought of as useless. Wonderful! Marvellous! This is the Lord's doing. It is marvellous in our eyes. This is the day which the Lord has made; let us rejoice and be glad in it.

Perhaps we have experienced great days like this. And for Christians the greatest of all is Easter Day, the day on which the rejected and crucified Christ was raised to life again to be the foundation stone of the worldwide Church. 'It is marvellous in our eyes'! Never lose the wonder of this, not even if your prayer time happens to be in the train or lying in a sick-bed. There is wonder at the heart of our faith.

A prayer

Lord, you are a God who does marvels. Open my eyes to see them, sometimes in the most unexpected places.

Praise and thanksgiving

I will magnify thee, O God, my King: and I will praise thy Name for ever and ever. Every day will I give thanks unto thee: and praise thy Name for ever and ever. Great is the Lord, and marvellous, worthy to be praised: there is no end of his greatness. One generation shall praise thy works unto another: and declare thy power. As for me, I will be talking of thy worship: thy glory, thy praise, and wondrous works: So that men shall speak of the might of thy marvellous acts: and I will also tell of thy greatness.

O David, we have had enough of your laments, complaints and calls for God's vengeance (mark that, by the way, David would not *himself* take the vengeance). Can't we have some rousing songs of praise from you? Didn't you ever shout for joy and revel in song at the glorious wonders of nature? Of course you did. No man, no woman, has genuine religious faith in the real God, the Creator and Redeemer, who doesn't lift up his heart and 'sing'. There must be praise and thanksgiving. And Psalms must be *sung*.

My guess is David's Psalms of praise were so buoyant, so uplifting, they become incorporated into the congregational worship of the temple worshippers. This is why the Hallelujah Psalms, and those like them, appear for the most part towards the end of the Psalter. David's original compositions have been added to and edited and grouped with Psalms deriving from later historical periods than David's. But the roots are Davidic. David did magnify God, yes, every day. Read today's verses again. Perhaps David did actually compose them, who knows?

Isn't there always something for which to praise God, not least the loveliness of a summer garden? I can't be in mine just now, but someone has brought me this lovely basket of flowers. Praise the Lord, O my soul.

Prayer

Lord, forgive my croaky voice but accept the praises of my heart.

Cut down to size

O sing unto the Lord with thanksgiving: sing praises upon the harp unto our God; Who covereth the heaven with clouds, and prepareth rain for the earth: and maketh the grass to grow upon the mountains, and herb for the use of men; Who giveth fodder unto the cattle: and feedeth the young ravens that call upon him. He hath no pleasure in the strength of an horse: neither delighteth he in any man's legs. But the Lord's delight is in them that fear him: and put their trust in his mercy.

I am writing these notes in the garden and over the hedge are a couple of horses cantering up and down the field thoroughly enjoying themselves. And I derive great pleasure in watching them, especially a dappled grey with a long flowing tail. And I am sure God has pleasure in them because they are alive as he meant them to be alive, fulfilling the purpose, or will, for which they were created.

So what does our last-but-one verse mean? It is a warning to every one of us not to imagine that he does not need God, he has resources of his own. He has a powerful horse, indeed a number of horses to pull his ploughs, he has a tractor, a huge harvesting machine, and in the garage a shining Mercedes car ... What is more, look at his physical strength. Those powerful arms and legs! The breadth of his chest. He has resources to achieve anything. He needs the help of no one, thank you very much.

Doesn't he? What will all those undoubted resources avail him if God doesn't send the rain, causing the grass to grow which feeds the cattle by which he lives? He needs 'cutting down to size'. At the end of the day we all depend on God's mercy. They who recognize this dependence, yes enough to praise God upon the harp, tin whistle, or whatever, are the ones that delight God.

More singing then! If you read the Psalms you must be prepared to sing.

The motor car

O sing to the Lord a song of thanksgiving: sing praises to our God upon the harp. He covers the heavens with cloud and prepares rain for the earth: and makes the grass to sprout up on the mountains. He gives the cattle their food: and feeds the young ravens that call to him. He takes no pleasure in the strength of a horse: nor does he delight in any man's legs, but the Lord's delight is in those that fear him: who wait in hope for his mercy.

A few days ago a beautiful chestnut horse was ridden past my front gate with a girl on its back; nothing unusual about that! There are a number of riding stables in this part of the country, and almost always the rider is a young woman (why, I don't know). Now I know very little about horses, but even I could see this one was a beauty. What is this, then, about God taking 'no pleasure in the strength of a horse'? I am sure he does, for he is the Creator. He doesn't despise horses or their strength.

Let me make a suggestion. Substitute car for horse. Modern people often worship the car. People get judged by the car they run. Give a young man a powerful car and he feels twice the man. Sometimes a big car is bought for no other reason than to impress the neighbours or to make the customers of a business think it is doing well. Undoubtedly before cars were invented people adopted similar attitudes to the possession of a horse. But God isn't interested. Whether we have a big car or a strong horse makes no impression on our standing with God at all. What he looks for is the fear of him and trust in his mercy.

So with a person's legs (notice how careful I am over gender!). It is not our physical strength nor our beauty that ultimately matters, though they are not to be despised, for God the Creator is the giver of all. Our relationship to him determines the kind of person we are. So 'sing *to the Lord* a song of thanksgiving'—not to that impressive car, or beautiful horse, or those impressive legs!

A prayer

From the worship of our possessions
O Lord, deliver us.

Our foundation stone

Open to me the gates of righteousness, that I may enter through them and give thanks to the Lord. This is the gate of the Lord; the righteous shall enter through it. I thank thee that thou hast answered me and hast become my salvation. The stone which the builders rejected has become the head of the corner. This is the Lord's doing; it is marvellous in our eyes. This is the day which the Lord has made; let us rejoice and be glad in it. Save us, we beseech thee, O Lord! O Lord, we beseech thee, give us success!

Have I been rather too 'homely' in writing these notes on Psalms, lighting them up (I hope) with everyday illustrations to bring out the meaning for us now? Well, today, I am going to plunge back into Hebrew history.

First let me ask for your imagination. Behind this Psalm is the day when the Jewish people returned from their long years of exile in a foreign land. They laid a foundation stone of the new temple they were going to build, to replace the one that the invaders had destroyed. It looked a puny little piece of stonework set there on the site and the builders turned their noses up at it. Would there ever be a temple? Doubts were widespread.

But a temple was built using that humble piece of stonework in the foundation. And the day came for its opening and dedication. There was a grand procession and a gathering of priests there to receive it. 'Open to me the gates of righteousness, that I may enter through them and give thanks to the Lord' was the call. And the answer from within, 'This is the gate of the Lord; the righteous shall enter through it.'

And then this commentary in the light of all the prayer that had been offered up for this new building, the focus of their faith: 'I thank thee that thou hast answered me and hast become my salvation.' And then they looked at that humble little piece of original stonework now part of the foundation of the new temple. 'The stone which the builders rejected has become the head of the corner. This is the Lord's doing; it is marvellous in our eyes.'

Is it any wonder we sing this Psalm at Easter? Jesus was insulted, despised and crucified. Who would believe that a worldwide faith would be built on him as the foundation? But it has happened and it is 'marvellous in our eyes'.

Prayer

Lord, let the Church never lose the sheer wonder of the resurrection of Jesus. The foundation stone of our faith lies here. Let us clap our hands and sing. 'This is the day which the Lord has made; Let us rejoice and be glad in it.'

Public worship

Public worship of God is important. It is a matter of seriousness that in recent years it has suffered a decline. Standards of uprightness will not be maintained in the social life of the country if public worship falls into neglect. Discipline and regularity are required. We need to keep going to church even if it seems to be giving us little in the way of instruction, regrettable as this is. Worship can be uplifting and those responsible for conducting it should make it so.

It needs context, of course. It needs to meet the worshippers where they are. One of our basic needs is forgiveness. Worship brings this home to us. We know that as sinners we are not fit to come into God's presence. But then we learn that he is a gracious God and longs to forgive us, if we will only confess our sins and shortcomings be they great or small.

God takes away the barriers. More than that, through worship he sets our feet on the right paths. God's guidance is a reality. Sometimes the way ahead is straight and clear. At other times we come to perceive what we should do by means of little signs, as it were, by the roadside. Look out for the concentration on worship, forgiveness and guidance as you read the Psalms. They are never morbid, they do not dwell on our sins or exaggerate them. The aim is for us to come out into the clear, to be buoyant and confident. We shall make mistakes and at times we shall be cast down, but God will lift us up if we seek him. And do not forget that we are looking forward to the joy of his presence when this life is over.

Prayer

Lord, it was a bit of an effort to go to Church last Sunday. There was so much work to be caught up with in the garden and I didn't feel like singing anything after such a tough week at work. I was even tempted to reckon church-going a waste of time. I was wrong. We need the fellowship of other Christians to strengthen our prayers. We need to let our witness be seen in the neighbourhood as people see us making for church Sunday by Sunday. Lord, I pray for my local church, for its ministry, for its congregation, for both young and old. Make it a powerhouse for good in our community: kindly, charitable and wise. I pray for the whole Church in our country worshipping separately but more and more seeking to join together. Lord, strengthen the church-going in every area of the nation's activity: for the welfare and health of its life and for your glory. Amen.

Introduction to worship

But I through the abundance of thy steadfast love will enter thy house, I will worship toward thy holy temple in the fear of thee. Lead me, O Lord, in thy righteousness because of my enemies; make thy way straight before me.

I cannot read this Psalm without being arrested by verses 7 and 8. This is because verse 8 has been turned into a very beautiful introit appropriately sung before a service of worship. It brings back the memory of the choir of a church where I was vicar for nearly twenty years, lined up in the vestry with the doors into the nave barely ajar. The organ came gently to the stop finishing on one faint note which gave the cue for the choir to sing unaccompanied: 'Lead me, Lord, lead me in thy righteousness, make thy way straight before my face.'

The congregation could just hear it, as it were in the distance. Then the vestry doors were opened and the choir moved slowly to their places in the chancel. And before any hymns were sung we recited as a body the general confession. This was the beginning of our regular Sunday worship. Dramatic? Maybe. But it marvellously set the tone for our approach to God in worship. Certainly the Psalmist would agree. See verse 7. 'But I by your great mercy will come into your house; in reverence I will bow toward your holy temple.'

We ought not to barge boisterously into worship in church as if we had a right to be there. It is only on account of God's mercy that we are there at all, for God is righteous and separate from sinners (see verses 4 and 5). So we ask him to take us by the hand and lead us into his presence where first of all we kneel down and confess our sinfulness. And if we are sincere he will take us into his presence and our needs will be met. How glad we are that we came. God is our refuge from the trials and tribulations of life. We are able to lift up our voices and sing as best we can. And with the singing a prayer that God will protect all those who love his name so that they too can rejoice. The Psalm gives us this assurance and ends on a note of confidence (see verse 12).

Prayer

Lord, thank you for every occasion of worship that has been meaningful to me. Make it so for many others in need.

Not as we deserve

O Lord, rebuke me not in thy anger, nor chasten me in thy wrath. Be gracious to me, O Lord, for I am languishing; O Lord, heal me, for my bones are troubled. My soul also is sorely troubled. But thou, O Lord— how long?

Dear me, do we really have to read this Psalm? Look it up in the Bible and you will see that it goes on and on. 'I am weary with my moaning; every night I flood my bed with tears; I drench my couch with my weeping' (Psalm 6:6, RSV). Isn't this a bit much? Possibly it is, but suppose you live in Bosnia or Somalia? Suppose you have seen your house reduced to a pile of rubble, have lost your whole family, and you are the only one to have escaped? I am writing these notes in my study. The central heating is on, and there is a comfortable armchair for me to sink into when I have sat upright at my desk for long enough. I have also been well fed. What have I done to deserve this? The answer is, nothing at all.

'What have I done to deserve this?' is a question I have frequently had put to me when I have been visiting an ill person in hospital. The person feels terribly frustrated. Often all was going well until the illness come along. Judging from today's reading in Psalm 6 the Psalmist took what had happened to him as God's punishment; he felt he was being chastened for something he had done wrong. He hoped that God would soon stop punishing him—he had had enough.

But he had got it wrong. God doesn't treat us according to our deserts. That man I met with Parkinson's disease didn't deserve it. That other man who has never had a day's illness in his long life doesn't deserve it either. Changes and chances come to us all and we simply cannot work out why this happens to one and that happens to another. What we have to grasp is that God is with us always, he has not deserted us, and he is not paying us back. He doesn't pay us back. He is a God of grace, and if we will only turn to him trustingly he will 'see us through', perhaps in a way we never expected. Remember the whole human race deserves death for the mess we have made of the world, but Christ died and rose again that we might know eternal life. We don't deserve it—but we shall receive it.

A prayer

Lord, forgive me if I have thought of you as a hard taskmaster. Give me the grace to trust you both when the sun shines and when clouds darken the sky.

A royal Psalm

The Lord answer you in the day of trouble! The name of the God of Jacob protect you! May he send you help from the sanctuary, and give you support from Zion! May he remember all your offerings, and regard with favour your burnt sacrifices! May we shout for joy over your victory, and in the name of our God set up our banners! May the Lord fulfil all your petitions! Now I know that the Lord will help his anointed; he will answer him from his holy heaven with mighty victories by his right hand. Some boast of chariots, and some of horses; but we boast of the name of the Lord our God. They will collapse and fall; but we shall rise and stand upright. Give victory to the king, O Lord; answer us when we call.

This is designated a royal Psalm. That is a prayer *for the king*, not the king's own prayer. It is not, therefore, a Psalm of David, as some of the others have been, but a prayer by the nation for the king. It could have originated in a national assembly on behalf of David when he was established in the kingdom. What we have here is a clear recognition that the king's real strength is rooted in God, not himself. What is more, the nation's strength lies in its dedication *with him* to God. What is relied upon for survival as a nation is not finally chariots and horses (military might), whatever part they may rightly have to play, but in the solidarity of national dedication embodied in the king. Is all this too remote from the level most of us live out our individual lives? But it could remind us to pray for our leaders. Their faith, or lack of it, may be more important for our people's welfare than we realize.

Prayer

We pray for all the leaders of our nation.

A prayer for guidance

Make me to know thy ways, O Lord; teach me thy paths. Lead me in thy truth, and teach me, for thou art the God of my salvation; for thee I wait all the day long. Be mindful of thy mercy, O Lord, and of thy steadfast love, for they have been from of old. Remember not the sins of my youth, or my transgressions; according to thy steadfast love remember me, for thy goodness' sake, O Lord!

Here is a young man on a walking tour. Picture the scene. He makes his way through green valleys, he struggles up steep slopes, and feels his way carefully over little wooden planks under which the raging torrents of water plunge their way into the valley below. His pack on his back is heavy, and almost drags him to the ground. He knows his destination but often he does not know which turning to take when the path diverges. So, almost against his will, he is forced to call out to someone and ask the right way.

Like a path, life stretches out before us. We roughly know the way. We have negotiated some awkward places already and we reckon we can manage the rest. But the day will come when choices lie before us. Shall I do this or that? Shall I accept this job or that? Shall I trust this person or the other person? We never know when we shall find ourselves making these kinds of difficult choices. We had better get into the habit of calling on God at the beginning of each day. 'Make me to know thy ways, O Lord; teach me thy paths.'

One woman has told me about one of her memories from when she was a little girl. She often used to stay with her grandmother in the country. In front of the house there ran a stream in a deep-sided ditch. To go anywhere, it was necessary to cross it on a single plank while holding on to a rickety handrail. She was warned to be very careful, for if she fell in she might drown. She dreaded that stream, but one day she did cross it—gingerly putting one foot in front of the other. Gradually she gained the confidence to cross it more easily, but even in later life the initial fear never left her completely.

Even though we put our trust in God every day we mustn't be surprised if we are still a bit nervous. It doesn't mean we are poor Christians. It means we are still mortal.

A prayer

Lord, I am a nervous creature, but I do trust you.

God's house

O Lord, I love the habitation of thy house, and the place where thy glory dwells.

I know of a family who had to leave their home in East Germany. Not unexpectedly, they brought a picture with them so that they would always remember their past life. It was a modest little picture, but what was unusual was that it wasn't of the house where they had lived for years, nor of the village where it was situated. Instead it was a picture of a church—a very ordinary-looking church of no obvious architectural merit. Yet clearly this was the place that they loved most and that meant most to them. They never wanted to forget it.

Now the significant fact about this family is that they *belonged* to this church. There is all the world of difference between attending a church and belonging to one. We don't belong to a building—we belong to the people who worship there. The place is loved because of the people, and the love is brought into being, and kept alive, by the ministry of word and sacraments. So the place gets built into life and experience, and becomes part of the worshippers. They come to love it. They may treasure a picture of it, even though it may not be much to look at. And they may show their devotion to the place in practical ways—helping with the dusting, polishing the brass, keeping the grass cut in the churchyard, seeing that the notice boards outside are bright and attractive. One of the best ways to tell if a church is loved is to observe whether it is well kept or it is dirty and dilapidated.

Perhaps the Prayer Book version of this verse (Psalm 26:8) is helpful here. 'Lord, I have loved the habitation of thy house and the place where thine honour dwelleth.' We honour God by looking after his house. We dishonour God by neglecting its appearance.

Not everyone has a church where they feel thoroughly at home, and it may not be their fault. But if you have, then thank God from the bottom of your heart. This must have been true of W. Bullock and Sir H.W. Baker, or they would never have written this hymn.

A way to worship

If you know the hymn, sing this verse of it aloud. Otherwise just read it, then reflect on it.
We love the place, O God,
Wherein thine honour dwells.
The joy of thine abode
All earthly joy excels.

Over-confidence

I will magnify thee, O Lord, for thou hast set me up: and not made my foes to triumph over me. O Lord my God, I cried unto thee: and thou hast healed me. Thou, Lord, hast brought my soul out of hell: thou hast kept my life from them that go down to the pit. Sing praises unto the Lord, O ye saints of his: and give thanks unto him for a remembrance of his holiness. For his wrath endureth but the twinkling of an eye, and in his pleasure is life: heaviness may endure for a night, but joy cometh in the morning. And in my prosperity I said, I shall never be removed: thou, Lord, of thy goodness hast made my hill so strong. Thou didst turn thy face from me: and I was troubled.

Yes, David, things look pretty good for you now—all the Israelites have crowded to make you king in Hebron (2 Samuel 5); you have a fine house—how different from the holes in the rocks where you went for your life, Saul at your heels—and now Saul is dead and the neighbouring hostile tribes suppressed. You are king in deed and in name. To crown all this, in a brilliant military exploit you wrested from the Jebusites the hill of Zion, and it became Jerusalem, the city of David. What day could claim to hold more significance for history, the history of the world! Is it surprising that David took down his lyre, composing and singing the opening verses of this Psalm? If you can remember how to chant, sing them with him now, as I am singing while I write—you must sing the Psalms, they were written for singing.

But, O David, you (on occasions) short-sighted man! Because the sun shines on you today, you cannot count on its shining tomorrow. It may. It may not. And just as well, otherwise cockiness steps in and then the troubles multiply.

Prayer

In all time of our tribulation; in all time of our wealth: Good Lord, deliver us.

(from the Litany)

God guides his servants

But I trust in thee, O Lord, I say, 'Thou art my God.' My times are in thy hand; deliver me from the hand of my enemies and persecutors! Let thy face shine on thy servant; save me in thy steadfast love!

The verse that grips me here is, 'My times are in thy hand'. I have believed this for many a long year and still believe it. God prepares the way for those who trust him.

Let me tell you a story. More than fifty years ago a vicar informed his congregation that a mission was to take place in the town; some students would take part. He appealed for offers to put them up. Hearing of this a young woman told him of a couple who would help in this way but asked that a man, not a young student, be sent, but someone with ability to make out a case for the Christian gospel because the husband, a businessman, was showing interest.

I found myself billeted in that very comfortable home knowing nothing of all this.

About three days after my settling in, my hostess announced that she would like me to meet a very elegant young woman who had helped them in the Christian faith. Next day she ushered her into the drawing room. I was captivated. I admit it. And when on the sofa she asked me an intelligent question about a verse in the prologue to St John's Gospel, I was captivated even more. Not surprisingly we met again and two years later I married her. Then I learned that she it was, who, knowing nothing about me or even my existence, was responsible for my going to that house where we met.

For fifty-four years she supported my ministry. Not least she rescued me from being too 'booky' a Christian (I was a junior theological tutor at the time) and gently encouraged me to meet people in a parish. In a way therefore she made me. Are you surprised then if I tell you I believe in the guidance of God: 'My times are in thy hand'?

She died suddenly three weeks ago.

Prayer

Lord, forgive me if I ever doubt your guidance.

Confession

Happy the man whose disobedience is forgiven, whose sin is put away! Happy is a man when the Lord lays no guilt to his account, and in his spirit there is no deceit. While I refused to speak, my body wasted away with moaning all day long. For day and night thy hand was heavy upon me, the sap in me dried up as in summer drought. Then I declared my sin, I did not conceal my guilt. I said, 'With sorrow I will confess my disobedience to the Lord'; then thou didst remit the penalty of my sin.

Here is a man who is proud, wooden and stubborn. He knows he has broken one of God's commandments but he won't admit it. Or more likely he says to himself, 'Well everyone does it, why shouldn't I?' And if he is very sophisticated he argues along the lines that the lifestyle looked for from Christians in the New Testament does not apply in our different cultural environment. We know so much better these days how the human body and mind work. No there really is no sin to confess. But his uneasy conscience won't go away. It makes him miserable. And aspirins don't really help. Even his physical health is undermined when this inner unease drags on.

A bad case! Yes, no doubt, but even in mild cases of 'not coming clean' before God, prayer becomes a farce and worship barren. The remedy, however, is at hand. 'Lord, I did wrong…'

Then the sun breaks out again through the clouds. Whoever does not know what all this means cannot ever have really faced up to himself in the presence of God.

A prayer

Dear Lord and Father of mankind,
Forgive our foolish ways!
Re-clothe us in our rightful mind,
In purer lives thy service find,
In deeper reverence praise.

J.G. Whitier

Stubbornness overcome

Blessed is he whose transgression is forgiven, whose sin is covered. Blessed is the man to whom the Lord imputes no iniquity, and in whose spirit there is no deceit. When I declared not my sin, my body wasted away through my groaning all day long. For day and night thy hand was heavy upon me; my strength was dried up as by the heat of summer. I acknowledged my sin to thee, and I did not hide my iniquity; I said, 'I will confess my transgressions to the Lord'; then thou didst forgive the guilt of my sin.

Were you stubborn, David, I mean was there some occasion when you knew in your heart of hearts that you had done wrong, perhaps to a neighbour or a friend, perhaps to your wife? And you said to yourself, 'Well, it was his/her fault! What else could I do?' And you went about your day's work. And you joined in the usual meal that evening. You talked. You made jokes. You went to bed. All next day, David, you went about your work and your play. But all the time that thing you laboured to dismiss from your mind rankled. It hadn't really gone away... it was only smothered: you smothered it.

At last, however, your stubbornness broke. You got down on your knees and confessed to God that *you* had done the wrong. And lo, receiving God's forgiveness, a remarkable peace stole over your heart and you found the strength to put the matter right with the wronged party.

Old-fashioned? Unrealistic? Soft piety? I guess David would disagree with you. Otherwise, would he have written this Psalm?

Prayer

Grant, we beseech thee, merciful Lord, to thy faithful people pardon and peace, that we may be cleansed from all our sins and serve thee with a quiet mind.

Willing response

I will teach you, and guide you in the way you should go. I will keep you under my eye. Do not behave like horse or mule, unreasoning creatures, whose course must be checked with bit and bridle. Many are the torments of the ungodly; but unfailing love enfolds him who trusts in the Lord. Rejoice in the Lord and be glad, you righteous men, and sing aloud, all men of upright heart.

We don't like the phrase, 'torments of the ungodly', but think of it this way. Here is a man who has played the fool with his health. Overeating, over-drinking, chain smoking—not to mention some secret resource to drugs in order to pep himself up. He has to pay for this. Duodenal ulcers, alcoholism, lung cancer. The consequent pain can be tormenting. How can he be guided in the right way? If he is an unreasoning creature, and the likelihood is that he will become so as a result of these follies, he will have to be checked with stiff regulations, even some form of hospitalization. He will only go straight if he is held in like a horse or mule with a bit and bridle.

A far more sensible way to go about life is to listen to the words of wisdom which God has given us in the scriptures and to give a willing, not a compulsory response. We must understand that God guides us and teaches us in the way we should go *because he loves us* and longs for our welfare. He has no pleasure in punishment. He wants willing and loving obedience from men and women with a song in their hearts. One ounce of it is worth more than a ton of compulsion.

Prayer

Teach me, O Lord, the way of thy statutes; and I shall keep it unto the end. Give me understanding, and I shall keep thy law: yea, I shall keep it with my whole heart. Make me to go in the path of thy commandments: for therein is my desire. Incline my heart unto thy testimonies: and not to covetousness.

Psalm 119:33–36 (Prayer Book)

God's guidance

I will inform thee, and teach thee in the way wherein thou shalt go: and I will guide thee with mine eye. Be ye not like to horse and mule, which have no understanding: whose mouths must be held with bit and bridle, lest they fall upon thee. Great plagues remain for the ungodly: but whoso putteth his trust in the Lord, mercy embraceth him on every side. Be glad, O ye righteous, and rejoice in the Lord: and be joyful, all ye that are true of heart.

What would we think of a father or mother who gave no guidance to their children at all? Not much! But some parents hardly give any. It was fashionable a few years back to let the children bring themselves up. The results tell how wrong this is. So how can God be a wise and compassionate father if he gives no guidance to us his children?

But how does God guide us? By arresting incidents or signs? Through an opportunity presenting itself to us out of the blue—or an untoward accident to warn us not to go this way, not to take this step? Such striking incidents sometimes operate as God's guidance. We are not to rule out this possibility. Predominantly, however, God's guidance is less spectacular. God gives us guidance how to live through the Bible. There are examples of inspiring behaviour and of repelling behaviour. There are also definite instructions, notably the Ten Commandments, eight of them prohibitions. This is where we grow stubborn like a horse or mule. We resist checks on what we wish to do, and in doing so show ourselves to have no understanding. There have to be checks. At certain points life has to be hemmed in and kept on a tight rein or the result is chaos. Even a garden goes wild without cutting back. We have a way nowadays, however, of neutralizing the guidance God gives in the scriptures, Old Testament and New. We say it is 'culturally conditioned', so that what we read about human behaviour in the Bible no longer applies.

A prayer

Lord, make us more teachable in the presence of your word, so that we can receive your guidance.

Adultery

Have mercy on me, O God, according to thy steadfast love; according to thy abundant mercy blot out my transgressions. Wash me thoroughly from my iniquity, and cleanse me from my sin! For I know my transgressions, and my sin is ever before me. Against thee, thee only, have I sinned, and done that which is evil in thy sight, so that thou art justified in thy sentence and blameless in thy judgment.

Yes, David, the night was hot, and you were exhausted with the never-ending problems of state; and God knows, your home gave you scant pleasure. Then this woman came into your vision washing herself on her roof-top. What a figure! Rounded limbs! Jet black hair framing the whiteness of her skin! O the sheer delight of taking her in your arms. But, David, she is the wife of Uriah the Hittite on active service in your army! You didn't think of that did you? Or if you did mounting voluptuousness pushed it from your mind. You lay with Bathsheba.

And then things went wrong. Bathsheba declared she was with child, his child. For the sake of his reputation David must make it appear that this was Uriah's child, but Uriah had not slept with Bathsheba that fateful hot night! David was desperate. Uriah must be liquidated. And so David ordered his commander-in-chief to set Uriah in the forefront of the hottest battle where he would be killed, and he was. So now, David, you have not only adultery on your hands, but murder as well. And you are the Lord's Anointed!

Was there a way out of this impasse?

Is there ever a way out? No, not if we reckon adultery does not matter. It's commonplace today. But there is a way out through the gate of confession that adultery is a sin *against God*. God does forgive *and* cleanse.

Prayer

Lord, forgive me the weakness of my flesh.

77

A bad lapse

Be gracious to me, O God, in thy true love; in the fullness of thy mercy blot out my misdeeds. Wash away all my guilt and cleanse me from my sin. For well I know my misdeeds, and my sins confront me all the day long. Against thee, thee only, I have sinned and done what displeases thee, so that thou mayest be proved right in thy charge and just in passing sentence.

Something has gone badly wrong here. Traditionally this penitential Psalm has been though to come from the pen of King David after his lapse into an adulterous relationship with Bathsheba, the wife of Uriah the Hittite—not a pretty story! It contains the usual 'cover-ups' which accompany this kind of sin—for a sin the doer of it accounted it to be. That is something. It is a great deal. If sin is not acknowledged there can be no forgiveness. But where there is acknowledgement we can be sure the sinner is not rotten right through.

So don't write any man or woman off for one bad lapse.

Read the Psalm again. The words that stand out are: 'Against thee only have I sinned'. Well, what about the woman? Hasn't he pulled *her* down?—even if she did have a hand in pulling *him* down! And what about the woman's husband? Hasn't he been sinned against? But David—if it was David—sees his adultery as a sin *against God*. All of which must mean that he was a man very conscious of the presence of God in and around his life. It was God he had offended in the first place in taking another man's wife into his bed. And God judges rightly. Read the last line again.

Remember before God

those who have made a shipwreck of their marriage, children from broken homes, parents anxious about teenage sons and daughters, leaders of public life who mould opinions, the Church's witness to what God requires.

Cleansing

In iniquity I was brought to birth and my mother conceived me in sin; yet, though thou hast hidden the truth in darkness, through this mystery thou does teach me wisdom. Take hyssop and sprinkle me, that I may be clean; wash me, that I may become whiter than snow; let me hear the sounds of joy and gladness, let the bones dance which thou hast broken. Turn away thy face from my sins and blot out all my guilt.

Please bear with a little explanation in respect of these verses. Taken simply as they stand the words 'my mother conceived me in sin' could look like a sweeping condemnation of all sexual relationship, not least within secure marriage. It is as if David were saying, 'Don't blame me for my adultery—didn't we all come into the world that way?' But sex is not counted a dirty thing in the Bible. It is a God-given instinct. We cannot, however, fool around with it or we are in trouble.

Nor is David excusing his simple act by a reference to original sin, as much as to say, 'I can't help being a sinner, every one of us is caught in a network of sin by reason of heredity, the whole tree of humanity is defective.' No, there are no excuses here, quite the reverse. He is saying, 'Yes, I have committed a sin against God, but if only you knew, I am worse than you think. I've been like that ever since I was born.'

Prayer

Lord, I give up. I give up trying to justify myself, even though I know I am no scoundrel. But I admit that all along, ever since I was born, I keep on falling below what I would like to be, and want to be, but somehow I can't be. Cleanse me, Lord. Clean up my mind, my waking mind, my half-waking mind. Give me a new start. I know you will if I trust you.

A pure heart

Create a pure heart in me, O God, and give me a new and steadfast spirit; do not drive me from thy presence or take thy holy spirit from me; revive in me the joy of thy deliverance and grant me a willing spirit to uphold me. I will teach transgressors the ways that lead to thee, and sinners shall return to thee again.

Whoever it was (David?) who wrote this Psalm, or this part of it, had gone badly 'off the rails', as we say. Sometimes even the best of people 'come a cropper'. Then the way back—and there certainly is a way back to a right standing with God—is via repentance (which isn't the same as remorse or owning up to having been a fool) *and* receiving the forgiveness of God. Humbling? Of course! But it is the way. This writer, however, looked further ahead. He had no wish to 'come a cropper' again. He had had enough of the consequences, namely a sort of sickness inside, almost physical. He reckoned what he needed was *a pure heart.* So he prayed God for it.

What is 'a pure heart'? We know what it is to be hard-hearted, heartless, heartfelt and hearty. We can understand a 'broken heart', but what is a pure heart? I can only suggest, a heart which 'suffereth long and is kind' ... that 'beareth all things, believeth all things, hopeth all things, endureth all things'. Such is a Christlike heart. And we can't work it up. We can only pray for it and keep our Lord in view.

Prayer

Lord, I don't want to fall down again, you know I don't. Please regard my heart's wishes and not my achievements. I know you do not look on the outward appearance, you look upon the heart. But I confess, I am afraid, because I do not always hold to the right path. Create a pure heart in me, O God and give me a new and steadfast spirit: in the name of Jesus Christ our Lord.

A wounded heart

O Lord God, my deliverer, save me from bloodshed, and I will sing the praise of thy justice. Open my lips, O Lord, that my mouth may proclaim thy praise. Thou hast no delight in sacrifice; if I brought thee an offering, thou wouldst not accept it. My sacrifice, O God is a broken spirit; a wounded heart, O God, thou wilt not despise. Let it be thy pleasure to do good to Zion, to build anew the walls of Jerusalem. Then only shalt thou delight in the appointed sacrifices; then shall young bulls be offered on thy alter.

We come to God through our wounds or we don't come at all. Our sins make wounds. And sometimes God has to rub salt into them to cleanse them before he can heal them. The worst situation is to have untreated wounds, wounds left to fester. And it isn't only sins that make wounds, a 'let down' can do it, a lost love, or a failure. And if the almost inevitable wound called bitterness isn't treated, troubles will be set up. God heals wounds. And when we have offered him, as a sacrifice, our wounded heart and broken spirit, our other offerings will be acceptable. This is what our reading today says. We shall of course have to *decodify* the bit about offering young bulls upon God's altar! But this is often necessary in dealing with poetry.

Prayer

Open my lips, O Lord, that my mouth may proclaim thy praise. I don't want to labour my sins, my weaknesses or even my wounds. I want to be a joyful Christian, someone with a light in the eye, and a song in the heart; and to make lights and songs in other people's hearts. With thanksgiving and praise therefore, O Lord, I accept your forgiveness. I can scarcely believe it, but I do. I see the price you paid at Calvary. What can I do but accept?

Salvation history

Israel also came into Egypt: and Jacob was a stranger in the land of Ham. And he increased his people exceedingly: and made them stronger than their enemies; Whose heart turned so, that they hated his people: and dealt untruly with his servants. Then sent he Moses his servant: and Aaron whom he had chosen. And these shewed his tokens among them: and wonders in the land of Ham . . . For why? he remembered his holy promise: and Abraham his servant. And he brought forth his people with joy: and his chosen with gladness; and gave them the lands of the heathen: and they took the labours of the people in possession; that they might keep his statutes: and observe his laws.

Read these verses out loud and make a slight pause at the colon in the middle of each sentence, then you will hear that this is not flat factual history; history certainly, but history with a lift in it. The Psalms are lyrical, they were composed to be sung, some with massed choirs and orchestras in the temple. Perhaps I ought to have written not 'Read these verses out loud', but, 'Sing them out loud.' I had a go myself but I am glad you could not hear me. But do not miss the point. This is history to sing about. It is a special kind of history. It is salvation history, the history of what God has done for his people.

You have a salvation history and so have I. We have been brought out of darkness into the light of Christ. Maybe the event or series of events could not be labelled dramatic, certainly not in my case, but the new life is real enough. And other people had a hand in it. We had our Moses and Aaron. Mine was a clergyman in the town where I grew up. I could easily forget all about it. I have moved into different pastures since them, but not to remember my salvation history would be quite wrong.

Israel was not allowed to forget what God had done for his people. They were given these Psalms to sing. And before you put these notes away see how Abraham comes in again! Their faithful forebear was not to be forgotten.

A prayer

Lord, thank you for the light of life which you have granted me; and for those men and women who have let it shine my way.

Our forgetfulness

We have sinned with our fathers: we have done amiss, and dealt wickedly. Our fathers regarded not thy wonders in Egypt, neither kept they thy great goodness in remembrance: but were disobedient at the sea, even at the Red sea. Nevertheless, he helped them for his Name's sake: that he might make his power to be known. He rebuked the Red sea also, and it was dried up: so he led them through the deep, as through a wilderness. And he saved them from the adversary's hand: and delivered them from the hand of the enemy.

What had 'the children of Israel' (as the Hebrews were called) done that this strongly-worded confession should be on their lips?—'we have done amiss, and dealt wickedly'. Treachery? Bloody slaughter of their enemies? Rebellion? No, their sin was that they had forgotten all that God had done for them and ceased even to feel gratitude. This does not sound too offensive. It simply tells of a lack, an insensitiveness, a kind of woodenness. Almost every day we read in the newspaper of some appalling misbehaviour—murder, rape, embezzlement, vandalism. As regular Bible readers we are unlikely to be mixed up in this kind of gross misconduct. Through sheer familiarity, however, we could by now take the cross of our Lord Jesus Christ for granted. Perhaps once, maybe years ago, we were full of gratitude for what he achieved there for us—openness to the very heart of God, sins wiped away, the gift of eternal life ... but now all this has become stale, or at best the stock-in-trade of ecclesiastical liturgy. Our hearts are no longer warmed as once they were.

Now read today's verses again. What about God when we forget what he has done for us? And not only in the cross and passion but in a thousand lesser ways as well. We do well to recognize him as a God of grace.

I guess when the temple choir came to sing this Psalm all the stringed instruments were muted and the trumpets and cymbals silent or at least muffled. Don't forget this. In our worship we must have some solemn music as well as joyful. Why? Because we have sinned.

A prayer

Lord, I didn't mean to grow cold and callous but at times I have been. Forgive me, Lord.

God shows us the way

Thy statutes have been my songs in the house of my pilgrimage. I remember thy name in the night, O Lord, and keep thy law. This blessing has fallen to me, that I have kept thy precepts.

I don't like the word 'precepts' here, though I think it is an improvement on 'commandments' which is the word in the Prayer Book version. God does not *command* us after the fashion of a sergeant-major. This is not his way. Rather he shows us how we should proceed in life if we are to make a success of it.

The other day I stood looking at a piece of antique furniture called a court cupboard. It was made of heavy oak and was more than three hundred years old. Every part of it was ornately carved and inlaid with faces and diagrams. I tried to imagine the carpenter who had made it. He could have been no ordinary carpenter. There must have been an expert designer-craftsman and one or more skilled craftsmen who actually carried out the work. Now this is the point I wish to make—he did not stand over them and *command* them what to do; he instructed them, he guided them and *showed* them how to proceed in order to achieve the desired results.

This is how we should understand the word 'precepts' or 'commandments' in Psalm 119. God *shows* us how to live our lives and achieve the best. And of course he shows us pre-eminently in Jesus Christ. He is saying, 'Look this is the way. Do it like this.' Did he not say, 'I am the way, the truth and the life'? He is our example. He is not our commander. It is for the Christian to lean on him and take him as our example, for we have been redeemed by him. And maybe it is worth remembering that Jesus was once a carpenter. Perhaps he made cupboards!

Prayer

Teach me thy ways, O Lord that I may fulfil my life.

Learning the hard way

**It is good for me that I have been in trouble: that I may learn thy statutes.
The law of thy mouth is dearer unto me: than thousands of gold and silver.**

It is very curious how some verses of the Bible stick in the mind. For me the first verse in today's reading is one of them. I was aged about fourteen when I heard it as the text of a sermon. The church where I helped in the choir (I won't put it more strongly!) provided a strong pulpit ministry, concentrating to a large extent on the future kingdom of God—and I think I got a bit tired of it.

Then one Sunday there was a different preacher in the pulpit, which was quite unusual. I can see him now—elderly, and a great bulk of a man. I suppose he caught my attention because in the vestry before the service he told us he had been a boxer. Bluntly he called out his text, 'It is good for me that I have been in trouble that I might learn thy statutes.' I have never forgotten it. I wondered what troubles and scrapes he had been in.

Some people never seem to learn from what has happened to them. Over and over again they make the same blunders and do the same silly things. And not one of us will go through life without making some mistakes, but what we can do is learn from them. Some people shrug them off: 'It's just one of those things.' Or they say they couldn't help it—they just happen to be 'made that way'. Or they push all the responsi-bility on to an unfavourable environment.

The right reaction is to look the failing straight in the face and ask, 'What can I learn from this?' This is learning the hard way—but it's the way to develop a strong, independent character. And if through it all we come round to seeing that God's laws for living really are the best, then that mistake which we made won't have been wasted.

A prayer

Lord, looking back I wish I could have acted in a better way than I did. I could have been more kind. I could have been less selfish. Give me the grace and the wisdom to learn from my mistakes and not to harp on them now and spoil the present.

Coming back

Thy hands have made me and fashioned me: O give me understanding, that I may learn thy commandments. They that fear thee will be glad when they see me: because I have put my trust in thy word.

What had the Psalmist been up to that he should write these lines? Had he been drinking too much? Certainly not smoking because it hadn't been invented in his day. But 'burning the candle at both ends', perhaps. Or maybe he was a workaholic. Or stuffing himself at mealtimes and between meals. That is to say, had the Psalmist made the mistake of thinking he could push his body as he liked, because it was his anyway? But is this so? Has not God made each one of us and fashioned us? And has not God given us rules for keeping what is his in good condition?

The Psalmist had a lapse. Perhaps normally he was a tall, muscular fellow, full of strength and energy. There was nothing he reckoned he could not do. So he 'went the pace'. He became bleary-eyed, his hands shaky, he began dodging serious work. His friends shook their heads at the sight of him. Poor old so-and-so. And you, my readers, think I am making all this up, whereas I have a churchman in mind. He used to be upright, good-looking and respected for his ability, but not now.

And then the Psalmist came back. He accepted his troubles as God's judgment for disobeying his rules for healthy living. 'I know,' he wrote, 'that thy judgements are right and that thou of very faithfulness has caused me to be troubled' (Psalm 119:75). And when his God-fearing friends saw his recovery they rejoiced. So he wrote, 'They that fear thee will be glad when they see me because I have put my trust in thy word.'

A prayer

Lord, I would like my health of body and mind to be a witness to the wisdom of heeding your commandments.

The Word of God

Lord, what love have I unto thy law: all the day long is my study in it. Thou through thy commandments hast made me wiser than mine enemies: for they are ever with me. I have more understanding than my teachers: for thy testimonies are my study. I am wiser than the aged: because I keep thy commandments. Through thy commandments I get understanding: therefore I hate all evil ways.

When I was young, the Bible was more of a study book for me than a guide to my personal life, though I held on to one or two texts, such as 1 Corinthians 1:9: 'God is faithful through whom you were called into the fellowship of his Son Jesus Christ.' This was at a time of uncertainty about what to do with my life. I wrote the text out in Greek. My brother, who knew no Greek, made a beautiful copy of the words and framed them. They hung in my room for years. I still have them. I still hang on to them.

My study of the Bible developed in Hebrew, Greek, literary criticism, historical background and much else. Then I left academicism, though still valuing it, and met *people*—their hopes, their fears, their longings, their loves and their laughter. And I learnt that the Bible speaks to people in all the variety of these situations. More exactly, God speaks to them, as he speaks to us, *through* the Bible. So it becomes the word of God. That is how I came to know the Bible as a living book. I know it still as such and it holds my attention, not only of mind but of heart.

To be honest I can't write as fulsomely about love of the Bible as the writer of Psalm 119. 'All the day long is my study in it.' Not quite anyway. I have the grass to cut and some household duties. They take time. But every day I read a portion of the Bible, and dare to say it gives me more light and wisdom for living than all the other teachers to which I am indebted.

A prayer

Lord, bless those men and women who opened up for me your Word of Life.

Church-going

I was glad when they said to me, 'Let us go to the house of the Lord!'

I have a friend who taught me two lessons about Sunday: Sunday as a *witness* and Sunday as an *anchor*. As an ordained Christian minister I took Sunday for granted. It was the day for Christian service in the form of worship—though there was plenty to be done on other days of the week as well. But my friend is not a clergyman. She is a civil servant, and for many years she has held a responsible post in which she has met all sorts of people, some of them very high-powered. In all the time I have known her I have noticed that she never missed attending at least one church service every Sunday. There was the weekend when she was required to attend an important meeting in a remote part of Scotland. There was no provision for worship for the delegates present—so she had an excellent excuse to cut church. But she was up before breakfast looking for a church. She bumped into a military man also looking for a church, and discovered that he was a Roman Catholic. They each went their separate ways and found what they were looking for. There was another weekend when she was staying in one of the European capitals.

Her host and hostess were not church-goers but she asked them on Saturday evening where she could find the English church next day.

This allegiance to Sunday attendance at church in a natural and quiet way let those with whom she lived and worked know that she was a Christian. It was her way of witness in a secular environment.

Secondly, although she never said so, I think that her Sunday church attendance was an anchor. If she had let this go she might have started to drift—and, as anyone knows who has ever tried to sail a boat, that is dangerous. Not only because of unexpected hazards, but because it isn't easy to get back on course.

Even if sometimes we find church a bit dull, don't let us slip up on it. Remember church-going can at least operate as a form of *witness* and also as an *anchor*.

Uplifting worship

I was glad when they said to me, 'Let us go to the house of the Lord!' Our feet have been standing within your gates, O Jerusalem! Jerusalem, built as a city which is bound firmly together . . . Pray for the peace of Jerusalem! 'May they prosper who love you! Peace be within your walls, and security within your towers.'

It is almost impossible for me to read these verses without hearing in my mind the music of Parry's magnificent anthem entitled 'I was glad'. But a recording of the music, or even hearing it broadcast live over the radio, does not compare with actually being present when it is sung on some great occasion. It is the cathedral packed with worshippers— hundreds of individuals all united in one superb act of praise—that takes hold and lifts the whole congregation out of itself up onto a higher plane. This is what corporate worship should accomplish. And if we thought that attendance would translate this into a reality for us wouldn't we echo the opening words of this Psalm?—'I was glad when they said to me, "Let us go to the house of the Lord." ' Worship should bring us into the presence of God. It should also lift us up out of our little selves. Don't write this off as mere emotion. Religion without feeling is barren. It will accomplish very little.

And note this. Our acts of corporate worship on one day of the week will deepen our awareness of God's sovereignty and care over our lives *every* day and *every* week, busy as we may be with multifarious activities. I put one critical question therefore about an act of worship in church on Sunday. Was it uplifting? Will the impression still be there on Monday morning? Now be honest!

Read the rest of today's verses. The Church should be at unity in itself, division and quarrels kept at bay. We should pray for our church, our local church. God adds his blessings to all who care deeply about its welfare.

A prayer

Lord, we need more organists and choristers today, more musicians and singers, men and women of musical accomplishment and Christian dedication. Lord, hear our prayer.

Confession and absolution

Out of the depths I cry to thee, O Lord! Lord, hear my voice! Let thy ears be attentive to the voice of my supplications! If thou, O Lord, shouldst mark iniquities, Lord, who could stand? But there is forgiveness with thee, that thou mayest be feared. I wait for the Lord, my soul waits, and in his word I hope; my soul waits for the Lord more than watchmen for the morning, more than watchmen for the morning. O Israel, hope in the Lord! For with the Lord there is steadfast love, and with him is plenteous redemption. And he will redeem Israel from all his iniquities.

What has the Psalmist been up to? Has he let his wife down? Cheated his business partner? Committed a murder and got away with it? Or maybe nothing quite as lurid—just plain nastiness to someone. But whatever the trouble is, he can't forget it. It plays on his mind, and some nights it robs him of sleep. What can he do about it? The stereotyped answer is, 'Confess your sins and you will be free.' This is true, but confess to whom? To yourself, perhaps, but it doesn't work, the thing goes on nagging. To God then, but somehow this seems too easy and doesn't feel very different from confessing to oneself. The odd fact is that to confess to God seems easier than to confess to one's fellows. All of which adds up to meaning that confession and forgiveness isn't a simple matter at all.

I wonder if this Psalmist wanted *someone* to whom to confess and then to hear from him God's declaration of forgiveness. Did he lie awake at night longing for the morning when he could hurry around to the temple, find a priest and pour out his story, and hear from his lips the words of absolution? Then he would be all right. Of course confession and absolution can be abused, and can become a clockwork routine. But confessions are sometimes desperately needed.

No Christian can count forgiveness as coming cheap, not when he makes his confession in the presence of Christ crucified. But forgiveness really is there, for our Lord has paid the price.

A prayer

Lord, you forgave the men who crucified you. You will forgive me. Praised be your holy name.

Freedom from sins

Out of the depths have I called to thee, O Lord; Lord, hear my cry. Let thy ears be attentive to my plea for mercy. If thou, Lord, shouldest keep account of sins, who, O Lord, could hold up his head? But in thee is forgiveness, and therefore thou art revered. I wait for the Lord with all my soul . . . more eagerly than watchmen for the morning. Like men who watch for the morning, O Israel, look for the Lord. For in the Lord is love unfailing, and great is his power to set men free. He alone will set Israel free from all their sins.

The trouble with sins is that they turn into habits if neglected. Then they wind round and round our thoughts and actions like convolvulus in the garden. Then freedom to develop is restricted. We are not all we might be. This is obvious in extreme cases like drug addiction, alcoholism and chain smoking. Health is undermined. But cruelty, dishonesty and greed can so gain a hold in people's lifestyle that they seem incapable of being anything else but cruel, dishonest and greedy.

So let us beware. We all sin one way or another—which does not mean everybody is as bad as everybody else. But we need to confess our sins and seek for God's forgiveness, which he readily gives. God alone can set us free, but we must cry to him, even from the depths.

Prayer

Almighty God, who forgives all who truly repent, have mercy upon me, pardon and deliver me from all my sins, confirm and strengthen me in all goodness, and keep me in life eternal: through Jesus Christ our Lord.

A prayer vigil

Come, bless the Lord, all you servants of the Lord, who stand by night in the house of the Lord! Lift up your hands to the holy place, and bless the Lord! May the Lord bless you from Zion, he who made heaven and earth!

There are two necessities if we are to make much sense of this Psalm, namely information and imagination. It can so easily roll off our tongues as mere words, well, mine anyway. The temple in Jerusalem was kept open all day, every day, for prayer and worship, but at night it was closed. Not only closed, but guarded. There was a temple watch. Before, however, the priests locked them in they called to them bidding them to lift up their hands in the sanctuary and praise the Lord. So these temple night-watchmen were not mere security guards. They were the servants of the Lord with a ministry to perform. They were to see that the prayers to God never ceased in the temple, neither by day nor by night. They were to be continuous. And with the call to these night-watchmen to pray there came back the answer to the call—'May the Lord bless you from Zion, he who made heaven and earth.' There is a reward for those who maintain the prayer service whether it be day or night.

This is not an activity most of us can engage in all day long. There are a thousand and one mundane duties to perform and I certainly could not possibly keep awake all night for prayer, not even one night! What this Psalm does for me is to remind me that throughout every twenty-four hours, always, I am in God's hands. He is the Lord and I am safe there. I acknowledge this even if I cannot always be expressing it in words. The best I can manage is a short reminder in the morning before I start work and in the evening before I go to sleep. But on the basis of this Psalm I believe God will add his blessings to this little service of mine, and yours too.

A prayer

We praise thee, O God, we acknowledge thee to be the Lord.

From the Te Deum (BCP)

Blunders

O Lord, I call to thee, come quickly to my aid; listen to my cry when I call to thee. Let my prayer be like incense duly set before thee and my raised hands like the evening sacrifice. Set a guard, O lord, over my mouth; keep watch at the door of my lips. Turn not my heart to sinful thoughts nor to any pursuit of evil courses. The evildoers appal me; not for me the delights of their table. I would rather be buffeted by the righteous and reproved by good men. My head shall not be anointed with the oil of wicked men, for that would make me a party to their crimes.

If you never 'go out and about', but pass all your life among saintly men and women, if you never find yourself in the company of people who 'swear like troopers', and tell smutty stories, if you never have to sit through entertainment which tacitly denies all the moral standards you believe in—then don't bother with this Psalm, it has nothing for you.

Imagine yourself at an office party. How will you react? If by constant protest, you'll be written off as a crank. Perhaps by silence; and if you have not hidden the fact that you are a church-goer and a Christian, then your silence will be eloquent.

Prayer

Lord, I don't want to be a pious prig. I don't want to be stuffy, self-righteous and smug. And I know that all that is vulgar is not wicked, but just vulgar, and tastes differ. But I want to side with all that is best in life, and I haven't always; sometimes through fear, sometimes kidding myself that I was so broadminded, so charitable, so wise. Forgive me, Lord, for my blunders. I am sorry.

God's little signposts

When my spirit is faint, thou knowest my way! In the path where I walk they have hidden a trap for me. I look to the right and watch, but there is none who takes notice of me; no refuge remains to me, no man cares for me. I cry to thee, O Lord; I say, Thou art my refuge, my portion in the land of the living. Give heed to my cry; for I am brought very low!

A youth group with their leader was trekking across the mountains when a thick fog came down and they completely lost their way, indeed all sense of direction. They decided there was only one thing to do, they must find the direction marks painted on stones and rocks to indicate the pathway. They broke up their formation and dispersed but making sure that no one was out of shouting distance of some other of the group. So they continued to search in the fog. Whenever one of them hit on a sign he called the others together and from there, with a similar action, they sought the next sign. So from one sign to another they groped their way through the fog and reached their destination safely.

There are times in the experience of most of us when we cannot go forward on account of the fog that hangs over our immediate path through life. We do not know which way to turn, which decision to make. We did not cause the fog. There was no need to blame ourselves. One concern only needs to occupy us in these situations—how to grope our way through. This is only possible by moving little by little, from one sign post to another till the fog lifts. The signpost could be the Sunday worship, the understanding of a friend who at least sympathized, even the few minutes of daily meditation perhaps with the help of a book as guide.

Keep a look out for *God's little signposts*; they tell us he has not forgotten.

Prayer

Lord, open my eyes to see.

God our support and stay

Life isn't a smooth run. Some bits of it—occasionally long stretches—mercifully are smooth. But there are bumps on the road, obstacles, diversions and sometimes accidents. If we are motorists we can insure ourselves against those, at least limiting the damage.

But what can we do about the journey of life? We can't insure ourselves against troubles of one kind and another, they are bound to confront us. We can, however, put our trust in God to carry us through. He will not always deliver us out of our troubles, but he will see us through them if we look to him. And it may be that we shall be better people for the rough experiences. We learn more of God the hard way, and our stature as persons is increased if we are all but broken sometimes but then with the help of God rise up again.

But we must consciously look to God. We must believe that he cares for us, and that nothing that can befall us is beyond his power. More than that, nothing is beyond his love. The writers of these Psalms (David did not write them all) had rough experiences of life and David was no exception.

It is the more surprising then that there are so many Psalms that tell of God as our support and stay. It is a wise man or woman who makes these Psalms their own. Psalm 23 will probably be familiar but there are a number of others it were well to commit to memory. This is my advice: make the Psalms your own. They will provide first aid when the road over which you must drive is bad.

Prayer

Lord, my life hasn't been easy, whose has? There have been rough patches, even some rough stretches, but I 'came through'. Let me not fall into the trap of writing them off with the empty phrase 'bad luck' or 'just one of those things'. The right course of action is humbly, quietly and prayerfully to seek the support of you, our heavenly Father, to sustain us in the dark days, not only in physical strength but also in mind and above all in faith. Lord, save me from being sorry for myself, from being aware only of my own troubles, with little concern for others, many in far worse straits than mine. Let me use the rough patches to become sympathetic to other people in their hard times, many far more painful than mine. Lord, give me grace to stand firm, to keep cheerful, and to be outward looking even in trouble, to your praise and glory, my support and stay.

At the end of the day

Answer me when I call, O God of my right! Thou hast given me room when I was in distress. Be gracious to me, and hear my prayer. O men, how long shall my honour suffer shame? How long will you love vain words, and seek after lies? But know that the Lord has set apart the godly for himself; the Lord hears when I call to him. Be angry, but sin not; commune with your own hearts on your beds, and be silent. Offer right sacrifices, and put your trust in the Lord.

David could scarcely believe it. He was still alive, still a free man, still the king with his faithful supporters around him. In exile yes, out beyond the Jordan river, but the immediate danger was past. But it had been a 'near thing'. Had Absalom heeded Ahithophel's counsel to attack before nightfall, David's army and his kingdom would have been in ruins. David breathed again. He breathed all day. Not that the danger was wholly past. His rebel son, Absalom, still commanded formidable forces. But at the end of this day of respite did he kneel to pray the words of this Psalm, words of thanksgiving to God, his real deliverer? He felt himself to be in God's hands, and he, for his part, had kept his trust. Why do so many people blasphemously reject this faith? Well might David ask! Well might we ask!

Prayer

Lord, I have had deliverance in my life, more than I know, certainly more than I deserve. Lord, from my heart I thank you. I thank you for each day's little successes, things that might have gone wrong, but went right. Lord, you watch over us even in the little things of every day. Praise be to you, the Lord and Deliverer.

How to go to bed

There are many who say, 'O that we might see some good! Lift up the light of thy countenance upon us, O Lord!' Thou hast put more joy in my heart than they have when their grain and wine abound. In peace I will both lie down and sleep; for thou alone, O Lord, makest me dwell in safety.

When I was about eight years old and my brother was ten, our mother packed us off to stay for a week or two with an uncle and aunt who ran a farm in Sussex. This was 150 miles from home. I still remember the first night. We lay side by side in a double bed and my aunt came in to tidy up the room. To her astonishment no tidying was necessary. My brother had a tidy little pile of clothes on a chair on his side of the bed and I had a similar little pile on mine. That is how we were brought up. We thought nothing of it.

I have since thought how good it would be if when we went to bed each night we made a neat little pile of the cares and worries that we have worn during the day and left them on a chair and went to sleep without them, trusting implicitly like a child in the loving care and watchfulness of God our Father. Does this sound childish? There have been times in my life when I never knew what problems demanding action would confront me on my desk the next morning. And if I hadn't wrapped them up each night, dumped them outside the bed and got a good night's sleep, I would never have coped the next day. I am not so hard-pressed these days, but I hope I have retained the lesson. Each night commit your concerns to a caring Father God and go to sleep trustingly. No, we don't always succeed. There is sometimes the awful waking up at four o'clock in the morning when everything seems black and hopeless. Try to remember then where you have dumped your worries. Don't wear your clothes—or your worries—in bed.

Read Psalm 4 again. Clearly, the Psalmist knew a source of joy in his heart that did not come merely from a good harvest of grain and wine and the resulting material prosperity. He believed that his ultimate safety lay with the care and watchfulness of God, and not in insurances, equities or bank balances.

A prayer

Lord, teach me how to go to bed each night as a Christian believer trusting in your fatherly care.

What we were meant to be

O Lord, our Lord, how majestic is thy name in all the earth! When I look at thy heavens, the work of thy fingers, the moon and the stars which thou hast established; what is man that thou art mindful of him, and the son of man that thou dost care for him? Yet thou hast made him little less than God, and dost crown him with glory and honour. Thou hast given him dominion over the works of thy hands; thou hast put all things under his feet.

I read through this Psalm in my study but the day was so lovely that I took my Bible out in the garden. A bird was obviously enjoying the day too, over and over again he sang his little song. Yes, it was easy this morning to rejoice in God's creation: 'O Lord, our Lord, how majestic is they name in all the earth.'

Perhaps David wrote this Psalm at night (the sun is not even mentioned in verse 3) or at least in the memory of those nights when he was a shepherd watching over his sheep in the fields. He looked up and marvelled at the spectacle of the full moon and the stars shining like lamps, great and small in the night sky (and they are particularly impressive in the Middle East). Yes, God's majesty really is visible in his creation.

But read on. Where do we humans come into all this? The Psalm says God thinks about us and cares for us. Yes, I like that. The thought will help me get along today. But what is this? 'Thou hast made him little less than God.' I have recently been catching up on my European history and feel like amending the Psalm to read, 'Thou has made him a little (only a 'little')

lower than the devil'! The terrible story of man's long *inhumanity* to man goes on and on today. What we see is *fallen humanity*. What the Psalmist saw however was man as he was meant to be—almost a god in the world, a surrogate lord (so to speak) of all creation. Sometimes he looks more like a destroyer of all creation!

But there came into the world one who more than fulfilled what we are meant to be, and in God's good time will be, through him who is our redeemer—Christ the Lord (Hebrews 2:6–8). That time is not yet, but meanwhile turn away from the troubles in the world, go out and look up at the full moon and the stars and, when day breaks, if you are fortunate enough, listen to that bird singing his heavenly little song: 'O Lord, our Lord, how majestic is thy name in all the earth!'

Prayer

Lord, we praise your name for all the wonder and the beauty you have given us. May we not only see it, but care for it.

We matter to God

For I will consider thy heavens, even the works of thy fingers: the moon and stars, which thou hast ordained. What is man, that thou art mindful of him: and the son of man, that thou visitest him?

I haven't anything very important to do today. I shall not be flying to Hong Kong to arrange some big financial deal, nor pleading someone's case in the Central Criminal Court, nor drafting some weighty memorandum for HM Government. Perhaps you will be occupied with activities of like importance with these. I don't know. But I shall dig in my garden. That is all.

So what interest can the great God who made the heavens and the earth, the moon and the stars, possibly have in my little life? And how can I presume to bring my petty problems in prayer to the divine Creator and Sustainer of the Universe? From the standpoint of time and eternity all my affairs, yes especially mine, are but a drop in the ocean.

So what shall I do? Curl up and reckon I am of no more significance than a summer insect born at daybreak and destined to die at sundown, its little life over? Not if I take Psalm 8 to heart. 'What is man that thou art mindful of him (Did you notice that?—'mindful of him') and the son of man, that thou visitest him? ... Thou makest him to have dominion of the works of thy hands: and thou hast put all things in subjection under *his feet*.'

I matter then to God. You matter to God. So much is this the case that he is mindful of us and visited us, notably in the coming of Christ to our world for our sakes.

So it is important how I go about today, even if I am only digging in the garden, and you too, occupied maybe on much more important affairs. And we can pray about them. God hears because we matter to him. Can we believe it? We ought to believe it. It helps us to lift up our heads and straighten our backs.

Prayer

Thank you, Lord, for letting me know you care for me.

Knowing God's name

The Lord is a stronghold for the oppressed, a stronghold in times of trouble. And those who know thy name put their trust in thee, for thou, O Lord, has not forsaken those who seek thee. Sing praises to the Lord, who dwells in Zion! Tell among the peoples his deeds! For he who avenges blood is mindful of them; he does not forget the cry of the afflicted.

Yesterday was a lovely day, so I forsook my desk and spent the time in the garden instead. Today is different, there is a howling wind, rain is pouring down. Isn't life a bit like that? There are smooth patches and rough patches. How do we react when we pass from the smooth into the rough? How do we react when we pass from the rough out into the smooth again? Read today's verses once more. They will tell us how King David reacted. He was back in Zion, what a mercy! But when the Amalekites and the Philistines were hounding him all over the country he wondered if he ever would be at home again. But it happened, and he lifted up his voice and sang 'Sing praises to the Lord, who dwells in Zion! Tell among the peoples his deeds!' This is how he reacted.

And this is the lesson he learned for the future, and we can learn. 'Those who know thy name put their trust in thee, for thou, O Lord, hast not forsaken those who seek thee.' I love those words and have made them my own over the years. I have had my rough patches and smooth patches too. I guess we all have, but even on the dark days for some people the clouds lift even then, those are the ones who know God's name. To know God's name is to know who he is,

to know his character.

Recently a lady greeted me in the supermarket. I was embarrassed as I couldn't remember who she was and felt I ought to know. She saw the look of puzzlement on my face and revealed her identity and where we had met. What a difference knowing her name meant! We chatted happily after that.

Do we know the name of God? Or is he only a traditional figure, reverenced in the sphere of religion? Perhaps God allows rough patches to crop up in our lives sometimes to drive us out of our religious formality so he becomes a living reality, one to whom we turn and trust; and he does not forsake us when we do. And when we enter into the smooth patches we will bear our witness as David did when the Philistines and Amalekites retreated. 'The Lord is a stronghold for the oppressed, a stronghold in times of trouble.'

Prayer

Lord, you are my refuge in time of trouble.
Let me never forget to hide in you.

God will answer

How long, O Lord, wilt thou quite forget me? How long wilt thou hide thy face from me? How long must I suffer anguish in my soul, grief in my heart, day and night? How long shall my enemy lord it over me? Look now and answer me, O Lord my God. Give light to my eyes lest I sleep the sleep of death, lest my adversary say, 'I have overthrown him', and my enemies rejoice at my downfall. But for my part I trust in thy true love. My heart shall rejoice, for thou has set me free. I will sing to the Lord, who has granted all my desire.

If you have never lain awake at night, unable to sleep, because something is on your mind, then shut the book, this Psalm is not for you. Well, not yet anyway, but perhaps one day it will be for you. I know, because I've been through this. The night seems endless, you long for the morning and when it comes you are so tired.

It was an enemy that kept the Psalmist awake. And everyone has enemies. Jesus had enemies and I expect they kept him awake some nights—and perhaps he lay there tossing and turning. I'll tell you what makes enemies—jealousy. That is the reason why Jesus had enemies.

Perhaps you are a really attractive looking person. Or perhaps you are doing really well at school or at college. And because people are jealous of you they are your enemies.

Or maybe what kept you awake at 4.00 a.m. was not some person or persons, but that pain in your back which never seems to 'clear up'. You wonder how you will manage the shopping.

'How long, O Lord, how long must I suffer anguish in my soul? Grief in my heart day and night?' And you pray for light, what you should do for light means life and dark means death.

I think Jesus prayed this Psalm. He prayed it on the cross, but not only then but also up on the hills of Galilee long before at night. He saw his enemies gathering in.

God answered his prayers and he will answer ours. And we shall start to sing. 'I will sing to the Lord who has granted all my desires.'

Now read the Psalm again and note the words 'How long?' four times.

A reflection

Do you know those lines of this hymn? 'I trace the rainbow through the rain, And feel that promise not in vain, That morn shall tearless be.' I have made that my own. Will you?

God does care

The impious fool says in his heart, 'There is no God.' How vile men are, how depraved and loathsome; not one does anything good! The Lord looks down from heaven on all mankind to see if any act wisely, if any seek out God. But all are disloyal, all are rotten to the core; not one does anything good, no, not even one. Shall they not rue it, all evildoers who devour my people as men devour bread, and never call upon the Lord? There they were in dire alarm; for God was in the brotherhood of the godly. The resistance of their victim was too much for them, because the Lord was his refuge. If only Israel's deliverance might come out of Zion! When the Lord restores his people's fortunes, let Jacob rejoice, let Israel be glad.

Who is this impious fool who says in his heart, 'There is no God'? The reference here is to a whole company of people, to be precise to the pagan people surrounding the little nation of Israel, God's people. In comparison with the way of life nurtured in the Law of Moses they appeared 'vile, depraved and loathsome'. God looks down from heaven and sees how widespread is the corruption. No one seeks after God, no one does anything good.

These unthinking tumultuous neighbours however have the impudence to claim 'There is no God.' Their taunt was aimed at Israel who claimed they were God's people and he would care for them. This, in the view of the neighbours, was nonsense. Because of this the Psalmist called them a fool (NEB 'impious fool'). The Hebrew word here is *nabal* which does not mean a simpleton but an impudent person. These pagan neighbours had the effrontery to declare that it did not matter one way or the other

if Israel trusted in God's watchfulness over them. There is no such God.

At first sight this Psalm seems to be saying that atheism leads to widespread corruption. But the concern here is with the denial that God does not care about people. He is not a caring God. He will not intervene on anyone's behalf, a nation or an individual. This is an impudent assertion. God does care. We live in his presence whether we are aware of it or not, and he is ready and waiting to come to our aid. To refuse to believe this is to be a *nabal*.

A prayer

Lord, I trust in your loving-kindness. Help me never to doubt this.

Take refuge in God

Therefore my heart is glad, and my soul rejoices; my body also dwells secure. For thou dost not give me up to Sheol, or let thy godly one see the Pit. Thou dost show me the path of life; in thy presence there is fullness of joy, in thy right hand are pleasures for evermore.

The Psalmist was desperately ill when he wrote this Psalm as we can gather from verse 1, 'Preserve me, O God, for in thee I take refuge. I say to the Lord, "Thou art my Lord; I have no good apart from thee."' He expected to die and fled to God for refuge. And deliverance came, and how it lifted him up! Now read today's verses again. His heart and mind were lifted up by an experience beyond his immediate deliverance from a deathbed to express his confidence in *a life beyond death*. Peter quoted these verses in his sermon on the day of Pentecost (Acts 2:25–28. See also Acts 13:34–35).

Did Charles Wesley have Psalm 16 in mind when he wrote that hymn we often sing at funerals, 'Jesus, lover of my soul'? It goes on 'Hide me, O my Saviour, hide, Till the storm of life is past. Safe into the haven guide, O receive my soul at last. Other refuge have I none, hangs my helpless soul on thee.'

When we feel desperately ill we need a refuge, something beyond the sympathy of friends, valuable and supportive though that is. But there are times and situations when the help of man no longer avails. How important then to have a refuge in God. Bereavement is such a time. People without this refuge attempt various devices to alleviate the pain. One is to go about life as if sleepwalking. Another way people try is to live in the past, raking up all the old memories. Yet other people try to take refuge in a frenzy of activities, or they try to drown their sorrows in drink.

All those devices are ways of running away from the situation. The one sure refuge is to hold on to the resurrection of Christ and the promise it gives of *life beyond death*, and of fulness of joy yet to be, and at God's right hand pleasures for evermore. Yes, shall be knocked about a bit, but not knocked down. We shall stand up again and lift up our heads— and even now and again our voices. Charles Wesley got it right, 'Other refuge have I none, hangs my helpless soul on thee.'

A prayer

Lord, grant me to keep your resurrection always in remembrance and not to be afraid of what lies beyond this life.

A cheerful spirit

I have set the Lord continually before me; with him at my right hand I cannot be shaken. Therefore my heart exults and my spirit rejoices, my body too rests unafraid.

I like these two verses and the way the Psalm ends—

Thou wilt show me the path of life; in thy presence is the fullness of joy, in thy right hand pleasures for evermore.

Here is a cheerful person, and it's good to have such people around. Gloomy people create gloom and cheerful people create cheerfulness. And this writer's buoyant spirit was not superficial. It did not depend on a sense of well-being after a substantial meal, fine weather or the prospect of an evening's entertainment—none of which is to be despised. On the contrary he knew what it feels like to be afraid in life, even of life. Perhaps his heart had been torn by losing the love of someone, and all his future looked bleak. Possibly a job had fallen through. Could he trust anyone again? Could he even trust God? These are the hurting experiences, and the galling questions.

But he came through. He smiled again, he laughed again. He joked again. All because he got a grip again on the conviction that had all but slipped through his fingers that God cares, and is always at hand, and has pleasures to give him even yet. God is no skinflint. This recognition lifted him up, not only one day, or two days but right on beyond the last day of life altogether.

Prayer

Lord, I do not know what today will be like, what joys will come my way, what sorrows may hit me. I do not know how well I shall feel, what depressing news will be broadcast, what burdens I shall have to carry. But this I know: I know you care and I know I am in your presence— the Lord, with pleasures to give for evermore.

A prayer in time of trouble

Hear, Lord, my plea for justice, give my cry a hearing, listen to my prayer, for it is innocent of all deceit. Let judgement in my cause issue from thy lips, let thine eyes be fixed on justice . . . Show me how marvellous thy true love can be, who with thy hand dost save all who seek sanctuary from their enemies.

As with the Psalm we read yesterday (Psalm 16) the Psalmist flees to God for refuge. This time the occasion is not a severe death-dealing illness but foes cornering him and making all manner of false accusations none of which could be sustained. This happens sometimes in life and godly men and women are not immune from this unjust hostility. Jealousy is often at the root of it. We are right then to maintain our innocence and uprightness of our conduct. There are times when we must resist injustice, but we do not, or should not 'pay back'. Notice how the Psalmist prayed: 'From thee let my vindication come.'

Then from the sordidness and shamefulness of his position surrounded by enemies he turns by contrast to the thought of God. And he does so in confidence, for he knows in his heart that he is not in the wrong. He even expects to see God's face so well is he aware of God's presence even in his present perilous predicament. Was it a vision that he looked for? We don't know, but whether or not this is some deep spiritual experience he believed it would give him deep satisfaction—far more than plain deliverance from his foes.

We ought to note what this Psalm is saying to us. Undeserved troubles may hit us hard but if we are in communion with God in mind and spirit those very dismal occasions may become the times when God becomes most real to us, we 'see his face' and experience a strange satisfaction in our inmost being.

A prayer

Lord, let me be conscious of your real presence even when my sky is covered with clouds.

God's care and keeping

Thou hast been my succour: leave me not, neither forsake me, O God of my salvation. When my father and my mother forsake me: the Lord taketh me up . . . I should utterly have fainted: but that I believe verily to see the goodness of the Lord in the land of the living. O tarry thou the Lord's leisure: be strong, and he shall comfort thine heart; and put thou thy trust in the Lord.

The other day I read this. A couple called their baby Immanuel (God with us), a name full of promise. He was always with them. They never left him. Something went wrong with his right arm and hand and he had to go into hospital, but still they did not leave him. He recovered and sat up again in his bed. But then something happened which puzzled them. He tried to draw his father's attention, desperately seeking to say the word 'Daddy', but failing utterly. At last, with his little left hand, which was sound, he held his bad right hand out towards his father. 'We did not know what he was trying to tell us,' said the parents. 'We never did know, although we never left him. But the day came when we had to leave him, for he died. And as he was lying in his bed, being prepared for his little coffin, we realised that this was the very first time we had left him alone. We found the thought all but unbearable—our little boy alone! And then some words from Psalm 27 came into our minds: "When my father and my mother forsake me: the Lord taketh me up." '

I had never thought of those words like this till I read this story, but I shall hold on to them more strongly now. Sooner or later we shall (as we say) 'lose' someone whose life is bound up with ours. What a comfort to know that they are not alone, the Lord has taken them into his care. They are not forsaken, they are not lonely. But what about us who are left? Now read the verses at the head of this page. They constitute a prayer that God will not forsake us in our loneliness and, even more, that we shall be strong and our hearts comforted.

Am I wrong to touch on this sombre subject in these notes? But do we not need to hear what God says through the Bible when our days are very dark?

A prayer

Lord, take me up
take those I love up
into your care and keeping.
I know you will.

My candle, your candle

Thou also shalt light my candle: the Lord my God shall make my darkness to be light. For in thee I shall discomfit an host of men: and with the help of my God I shall leap over the wall.

Did you know you had a candle? Every normal person has a candle. Here is a woman adept at needlework. Here is a boy quick to master new technological equipment. Here is a man able to do anything with animals. And a girl brilliant at the piano, and another with a facility for making friends. A housewife with 'green fingers'. We are not thinking about geniuses but ordinary people we encounter in the bus queue—yes, even the old woman just managing with two sticks. She has a candle. And God lit it.

Some people have more than one candle. In the parable of the talents which Jesus told (Matthew 25:14–30) one man was given five talents, another two, another one. For 'talent' read 'lit candle'. No blame attached to the man with but one talent but he got into serious trouble for not using it, or letting his candle 'go out'. Remember this, *God* has lit your candle, and mine (yes, I have one!) and the woman on the other side of my garden fence 'mucking out' her horses this morning. We are each accountable to God. He lit our candle.

If David wrote Psalm 18, and I think he did, he acknowledged that God had lit his candle, indeed more than one— marksmanship, music, poetry, the martial arts—and so he would not be imprisoned by the humble nature of his birth, he would 'leap over the wall', and he did. He became *King David* and even Messiah was called 'Son of David'.

Prayer

Lord, remember those with a gift but lacking the opportunity to use it. Give them a chance to keep their candle alight.

Learn to wait patiently

I waited patiently for the Lord: and he inclined to me and heard my cry. He drew me up from the desolate pit, out of the miry bog, and set my feet upon a rock, making my steps secure. He put a new song in my mouth, a song of praise to our God. Many will see and fear, and put their trust in the Lord.

I have had to cut back the hedges on the drive in front of my house to make more room for the car coming in and out. I am rather sorry about this, the green has all gone leaving clipped bare wood. Apart from ripping out the whole hedge and planting something else or installing a wooden fence there is nothing for it but to wait patiently. In time there will be a new growth and fresh green. 'In time' are the operative words. Anything to do with a garden requires patience. You can't sow seeds today and have flowers tomorrow. To be in a hurry with a garden is useless.

Is this a lesson we have to learn too in our relationship with God? As I write this note there keeps ringing in my head that lovely aria: 'O rest in the Lord, wait patiently for him and he will give thee thy heart's desire.' But we are so impatient in our modern world. We want instant results. Hardly has any event taken place than we want not only instant reporting of it on radio, television and in the newspaper, we want informed comment. We can't wait to see things in perspective. Speed is the key word today. Even new buildings have to be put up almost overnight. There is no time to settle, no time to take stock.

The Psalmist new better. Something had gone wrong for him. Somehow he was stuck, he just could not get going. And the place, or situation was not only desolate but depressing, it was dirty, a miry bog. And he cried out to God to pull him out and set him free. He was desperate. Even so, and this is the point to notice, even in that awful hole *he waited patiently* for the Lord. And his wait was not in vain. It never is with nature, nor with God. In due time the results appear, the garden greens over again, the Psalmist was lifted out of that dreadful hole and had his feet set on a rock.

And then he started to sing. It was a new song. I guess he lifted up his voice before he cleaned his muddy boots. And people heard him. They marvelled and what they saw and heard made them put their trust in the Lord for themselves. Let us hope and wait patiently for him, the God who will not let us down.

Prayer

Lord, we wait for the vision of your glory which we believe will come to us, for this is the message of Easter—resurrection and life.

God our refuge

God is our hope and strength: a very present help in trouble. Therefore will we not fear, though the earth be moved: and though the hills be carried into the midst of the sea. Though the waters thereof rage and swell: and though the mountains shake at the tempest of the same. The rivers of the flood thereof shall make glad the city of God: the holy place of the tabernacle of the most Highest. God is in the midst of her, therefore shall she not be removed: God shall help her, and that right early. The heathen make much ado, and the kingdoms are moved: but God hath shewed his voice, and the earth shall melt away. The Lord of hosts is with us: the God of Jacob is our refuge.

A few years ago I was being driven late at night in a small bus from Tel Aviv airport to Jerusalem. There were about twelve of us, a small party of Church leaders, Anglican, Roman Catholic and Free Church. Our driver was a Jew. Within a mile or two of the city he pulled in to the side of the road. We were puzzled, maybe a bit anxious, but we need not have been. With impressive pride he pointed to the illuminated walls circulating the city and said, 'There it is, the centre of the whole world.'

There was a time in the history of the Jewish people when they looked upon Jerusalem as their guardian. Nothing untoward could happen to them while the holy city (God's dwelling place as they understood it) remained intact. They were in for a rude awakening. Their mistake was to confuse a symbol with the living God. The Psalmist knew better: 'God is our hope and strength ... God is in the midst of her, therefore shall she not be removed.'

It is God's presence in the hearts of his people that is our final refuge—not the fact that we have church buildings dotted about the land. But if they are real houses of God, filled with people who worship, honour and obey him, then we can have the assurance that God is in the midst of us. We have a refuge and source of strength whatever storms rage and swell.

A prayer

Lord, we are sometimes fearful for the Church. Problems, dissensions among us and attacks from outside make us wonder what the future holds. Strengthen our faith that not even the gates of hell can prevail against your Church while we hold fast to Christ.

God comes in the storm

Our God comes, he does not keep silence, before him is a devouring fire, round about him a mighty tempest.

Last night we had gale force winds, the windows rattled, the last of the autumn leaves were swept off the branches, and, as a result, plenty of work to do in the garden clearing up. Is this how God comes to us? This Psalm says he does. And it is all so different from the idea of God as a kind of static ideal or a philosophic abstraction like 'the first cause' or 'the ground of our being'. God comes to us, he does not keep silence and our situation is shaken because of his action.

Perhaps we are disposed to question this. We think of God coming in our Lord Jesus Christ as the babe of Bethlehem. There was nothing tempestuous there. But wasn't there? The lives of Mary and Joseph were turned upside down. Herod, the king, we are told, was furious, 'hell bent' as some would put it, on obliterating this child. And Jesus' life as the man of Galilee was dogged by opponents seeking his life and finally a cross was erected to kill him in the most brutal way possible.

God is not a passive God, a God we have to search for under the rubble of our hopes and fears and disappointments. No, God comes. He comes to us most often in rough circumstances.

When I was for many years a parish priest in the West End of London caring for a congregation which on any estimate would have to be described as well-to-do, I remember visualizing the various members sitting in their seats in the church and wondering why on earth they were there. They had everything. What could they possibly need? And then I remembered how this one was suddenly bereaved, that one had a broken marriage, and that woman over there was eating her heart out with loneliness but too proud to admit it.

God had come to them in their storms of life. This is why they were in church.

Do you remember the gospel story of Jesus making himself known in a new way in a storm on the lake?

This is how it is. God comes to us when life is rough. Now read Psalm 50:3 again.

Prayer

Lord, I have had my rough patches, but you did not leave me alone. Praise be to thee, O Lord.

The strength to hold back

Be merciful to me, O God, be merciful to me, for in thee my soul takes refuge; in the shadow of thy wings I will take refuge, till the storms of destruction pass by. I cry to God Most High, to God who fulfils his purpose for me. He will send from heaven and save me, he will put to shame those who trample upon me. God will send forth his steadfast love and his faithfulness! I lie in the midst of lions that greedily devour the sons of men; their teeth are spears and arrows, their tongues sharp swords.

'For God's sake, men, keep still. Not a cough. Saul has entered *this cave* with a whole troop of soldiers. It is all up with us if you so much as dislodge a stone. He thinks the cave is empty. He certainly does not guess that we are here! Flatten yourselves against the walls. Your life and mine depend on it.' Is this what David whispered to his men in the cave whither they fled, and then, horror of horrors, Saul and his men trooped into the very same cave. Time passed. Then snoring. Saul had fallen asleep and his men retreated beyond the cave's entrance. This was David's chance. But what chance? To cut Saul's throat and end this ghastly chase across the mountains?

David did no such thing. Even under dire pressure he would not put forth his hand against the Lord's anointed who, for all his faults, he counted Saul to be. If he came one day to the throne, as he believed he would, there would be no royal blood on *his* hands.

So he merely cut off the skirt of Saul's clothing to teach him how close he had been to death, and that he was saved *by* *David* whom he had chosen to call his enemy!

A quite remarkable act. Given half a chance how often we hit back irrespective of who our assailant is.

Prayer

Lord, I don't always hold back when I ought to, as a Christian.

Rejoicing

Have I not remembered thee in my bed: and thought upon thee when I was waking? Because thou hast been my helper: therefore under the shadow of thy wings will I rejoice.

Someone said to me recently, 'When I went to bed I thought over all that had happened during the day and I reckoned how fortunate I was about what had come my way and how happy it had made me.'

There is wisdom in running over the events of the day as in the presence of God before going to sleep. 'In every thing by prayer and supplication *with thanksgiving* let your requests be made known unto God', wrote Paul to the Christians in Philippi.

There is always something for which to be thankful, even if only for a bed on which to lie! And when the new day breaks and the eyes are opened, let the first thought be of God's continual care through the coming day as well as through the past night. Why? Because God has been our helper, and will continue to be our helper. Knowing this we can face the dawn with confidence, and—who knows?—even sing, hum or whistle on the way to the bathroom: All will be well today. God will be with me.

Not that we can all be 'slap you on the back' types, though possibly such people have their place. Rejoicing 'in the Lord' in any case must not be forced. Perhaps it is most genuine when it is most modest. The hallmark is a look of contentment in eyes which do not quickly flare up into resentment. There is no more sure way of achieving this than by the habit of thanking God before falling off to sleep and of remembering his continual presence on waking up.

A prayer

Lord, you are good and gracious and you know our frailties. I am sorry if sometimes I fall asleep resentful and wake up fearful. I am sorry if sometimes I am a gloomy person, withdrawn, and complaining. Show me how to trust you, to rely on you, and to be thankful: I would like to be a joyful Christian.

A muddle

I think of thee upon my bed, and meditate on thee in the watches of the night; for thou hast been my help, and in the shadow of thy wings I sing for joy. My soul clings to thee; thy right hand upholds me. But those who seek to destroy my life shall go down into the depths of the earth; they shall be given over to the power of the sword, they shall be prey for jackals. But the king shall rejoice in God; all who swear by him shall glory; for the mouths of liars will be stopped.

Tradition has ascribed this Psalm to the strange incident that took place at Keilah in Judeah with its own lesson about human nature. The Philistines had attacked this city and robbed the threshing floors, which of course spelt hunger for the inhabitants. David felt God to be telling him to smite the Philistines, and save Keilah, which he did, in spite of his men's uncertainty about undertaking this risky venture. Then Saul stepped into the fray. 'God,' he said, 'has delivered David into my hands. He is shut in town with gates and bars.' David guessed as much and enquired of God if the people of Keilah would hand him over to Saul in spite of all that he had done for them. The answer came that they would, whereupon David with his six hundred men made a quick exit into the mountains.

What a muddle! Of what interest can all this possibly be to us? Perhaps our own life, however, is a bit of a muddle sometimes. We don't progress all the time in a straight line to the enjoyment of God's promises. Our path is often zigzag. Do not despair. God has not forgotten us, however odd sometimes even what we feel he has bidden us do turns out to be.

We must through manifold tribulations enter God's Kingdom.

Prayer

Lord, grant me and the whole Church the gift of perseverance.

The tongue and the heart

Come and hear, all you who fear God, and I will tell you what he has done for me. I cried aloud to him, and he was extolled with my tongue. If I had cherished iniquity in my heart, the Lord would not have listened. But truly God has listened; he has given heed to the voice of my prayer.

A notice in a delicatessen window read: 'Have you tried our tongue sandwiches? They speak for themselves.'

Perhaps you don't think that this is funny! Never mind, but it caught my attention because I have been reading the letter of James in the New Testament and he has a great deal to say about the tongue, our tongues, much of it rather frightening. 'Think of ships: large they may be, yet even when driven by strong gales they can be directed by a tiny rudder... So with the tongue. It is a small member but it can make huge claims... We use it to sing the praise of our Lord and Father, and we use it to invoke curses on our fellow men who are made in God's likeness... My brothers this should not be so.'

The Psalmist in today's verses used his tongue well. God was extolled with it. God's praises were on his lips (NEB). He had also banished iniquity from his heart. He had been in trouble and cried aloud to God for help and God heard his cry and did great things for him, so he used his tongue to call people to come and hear of his deliverance. This is what we have to note, the heart and tongue are connected. If our heart is thankful to God we shall use our tongues well. If our heart is angry with God we shall use it to do harm. It is possible to tell what a person's heart is by the way the tongue is used. There is such an instrument as a kindly tongue and such an instrument as an evil tongue. A kindly tongue can do an astonishing amount of good and an evil tongue can do an astonishing amount of evil. We have to be very careful with our tongue. This applies especially to Christian congregations. Churches can be ruined by gossip. There is a simple rule of thumb—if you can say something good about another person, say it, if not, hold your tongue.

And now what about the newspapers and news bulletins on television and radio? They seem to like to tell us the bad news which, let us face it, does exist. This is where we Christian people should come in. We shouldn't add to the world's sorry tale of woe by talking about nothing else. We should use our tongue to tell of good things, some of which have come our way.

Prayer

Lord, let the Church proclaim good news, especially the good news of Easter.

Full stature

I will go forth in the strength of the Lord God: and will make mention of thy righteousness only. Thou, O God, hast taught me from my youth up until now: therefore will I tell of thy wondrous works. Forsake me not, O God, in mine old age, when I am gray-headed: until I have shewed thy strength unto this generation, and thy power to all them that are yet for to come. Thy righteousness, O God, is very high: and great things are they that thou hast done: O God, who is like unto thee? O what great troubles and adversities hast thou shewed me! and yet didst thou turn and refresh me: yea and broughtest me from the deep of the earth again. Thou hast brought me to great honour: and comforted me on every side.

Some biblical texts seem to belong to us as individuals. We say, 'Ah, that is my verse. I love that one.' The first verse in today's reading is a bit like that for me. I was sitting in Fulham Palace Chapel on the eve of my ordination. I was nervous. I did not know what lay ahead. Would I be able to fulfil this ministry? Then the Bishop of London swept into the chapel, arrayed in purple. Standing there he said to us all, 'This is the verse for each on of you: "I will go forth in the strength of the Lord God and will make mention of thy righteousness only." '

This Psalm comes into its own when we have reached middle age and can look back and also begin wondering about the future. God has been with us all the way. We felt very small when we began but in middle life we seem to have achieved something. We are at our best when we reach our full stature. The past has made us what we are under God. But what about the declining years? The Psalmist worried a bit, hence the prayer

earlier in the Psalm: 'Cast me not away in the time of age: forsake me not when my strength faileth me' (verse 8).

A prayer

Lord, you have never let me go and never will. I will go forth still in your strength.

Declining years

Thou, O God, hast taught me from my youth up until now: therefore will I tell of thy wondrous works. Forsake me not, O God, in mine old age, when I am gray-headed: until I have shewed thy strength unto this generation, and thy power to all them that are yet for to come. Thy righteousness, O God, is very high: and great things are they that thou hast done: O God, who is like unto thee? O what great troubles and adversities hast thou shewed me! and yet didst thou turn and refresh me: yea and broughtest me from the deep of the earth again. Thou hast brought me to great honour: and comforted me on every side. Therefore will I praise thee and thy faithfulness, O God.

I stood waiting my turn in the baker's shop. In front of me a tall, grey-haired man asked for one Cornish pasty. He was neatly dressed. Carrying his tiny parcel with what I supposed was his lunch inside, he approached the exit. I held the door open, he looked so frail. 'No thanks,' he said, 'you go first. It takes me some time to manage the step.' I did go first. He was still negotiating the step when I reached the pavement . . .

Many of us will come to the time when we can no longer accomplish what used to be easy. This is hard. Understandably, it makes for irritation. We knock things over. We miss the kerb. We forget names. What we need to remember is that the faithful God who has brought us so far will not forsake us now. We shall cope with limitations, and success will be the ability to smile in that hardship. Cheerfulness is the great challenge of old age, and grumbling the besetting danger. There is one advantage of old age. We can look back *a long way* and see how God does guide those who trust him.

A prayer

Lord, if I fall in the street today or forget to order the milk I need, Give me the grace to laugh about it.

Any answers?

Thou shalt guide me with thy counsel: and after that receive me with glory. Whom have I in heaven but thee: and there is none upon earth that I desire in comparison of thee. My flesh and my heart faileth: but God is the strength of my heart, and my portion for ever.

Believing God does not mean we know all the answers to life's problems. Indeed, belief in God often introduces further problems. Only last week I heard of a young woman, married just four years, who has died of leukaemia. Her husband is heartbroken. Why does God let good people suffer? The Psalmist was tormented by another problem, the prosperity of the wicked. Mistakenly he thought he had found the answer. Soon or later God would cause these people to come to a 'sticky end'. But this is not necessarily so. Many of them live in comfort from their ill-gotten gains and die in luxury.

The trouble with the Psalmist's observation was that it was limited to this life on earth. The rewards of goodness and the judgments on wickedness came in the here and now—this was the recognized theology. All the more remarkable, therefore, are the verses in today's reading. The Psalmist lifted his thoughts to heaven. He gave up worrying about the insoluble problem of rewards and punishment. Instead, he contemplated his own position and made this remarkable statement, remarkable because he had no Easter gospel to inform him. 'Thou shalt guide me with thy counsel: and afterwards receive me with glory' (Psalm 73:22). Because he had come to trust God, he could live with his problems, even if he knew very few answers—all would be well.

A prayer

Lord, sometimes I get 'worked up' when I read of the dirty money with which some people have cushioned their lives. Give me the wisdom to leave these matters in your hands.

The life to come

Nevertheless I am continually with thee; thou dost hold my right hand. Thou dost guide me with thy counsel, and afterward thou wilt receive me to glory. Whom have I in heaven but thee? And there is nothing upon earth that I desire besides thee. My flesh and my heart may fail, but God is the strength of my heart and my portion for ever.

You must forgive me if you recognize some of what I write today as taken from my book on Psalms written ten years ago, but, you see, I still believe it!

The writers of the Old Testament had an inkling of life beyond the grave and reckoned we ought to live well in this life so as to win an immortality in the continuity of the race and in the memory of our children and children's children. In one or two places in the Old Testament however the thought rises above this and today's reading from Psalm 73 is one of them.

Here is a man who knows what life is (like me). The last thing he wants is the demise of the beloved. Rather he/she who loves longs to be with the loved one for ever. Very well then if God loves us— and isn't this what we firmly believe?— then it is quite inconceivable that he would allow us to be dead to him for ever. So Paul wrote in his letter to the Romans, 'For I am convinced that there is nothing in death or life, in the realm of spirits or superhuman powers, in the world as it is or the world as it shall be, in the forces of the universe, in heights or depths—nothing in all creation that can separate us from the love of God in Christ Jesus our Lord' (8:38–39, NEB).

Wonderful verses! And if we are safe in the love of God, and can't be anything else, those we love are also safe in that love and can never be lost *to us*.

Pity the Psalmist didn't know all this, but he got as far as he could in assurance about the future, and if he, why not us— who have the Easter gospel to tell us. The guarantee is in the phrase 'in Christ Jesus'.

Prayer

Lord thank you for every assurance of your eternal love, which never fails.

Little memorials

Then he led forth his people like sheep, and guided them in the wilderness like a flock. He led them in safety, so that they were not afraid; but the sea overwhelmed their enemies. And he brought them to his holy land, to the mountain which his right hand had won.

The Israelites were never allowed to forget how they were led out of slavery in Egypt, crossed the dry bed of the Red Sea and came to Mount Sinai on the other side where the Law was given to guide them. My guess is that some of them pulled up a stone or two from the sea bed and years after showed them to their children and said, 'Look, I picked this up from the floor of the Red Sea.' Wide-eyed, the children would finger them, then the whole momentous scene would live again in memory.

Do you have any of these little memorials? If you have, don't ever lose them or throw them away. They hold the important events in our lives. Times perhaps of great struggles through which we came, or some great kindness done to us by someone we never want to forget. And behind it all, the ever-present goodness of God.

Among the books that line the walls of my study are three or four that were presented to me. One is a reminder of the teachers in a school that we struggled to keep going—and succeeded. Another is of a congregation in one of London's West End churches. And two books are of very special significance for me. One is *A Manual Greek Lexicon of the New Testament* by Abbott-Smith. I see I wrote my name on the flyleaf on 6 November 1930. It cost me twenty-one shillings (now about £15). It took me nearly a year to save up that money for I only had three shillings a week. What memories that book brings back, and I still use it regularly. On the same shelf is *Young's Analytical Concordance to the Bible.* I was given it when I was a hard-up student on the condition that I went to fetch it on the other side of London. I did, but I only had the train fare to get there. Returning the several miles back was a problem, as the book was large and heavy. I started to walk, but after a few miles I was so exhausted that I sat down on a garden wall somewhere in South London. Then I struggled on to Westminster Bridge where for two pence I was able to pick up a workman's ticket for a train. I shall never be able to part with those two books.

A prayer

Lord, we remember the days that are past and praise you for your sustaining power.

The Lord is King

Do the bulletins broadcast daily 'get you down'? Is there any day when they don't get you down? We seem to lurch from crisis to crisis. It is hard to remember any occasion when something encouraging was reported. Gloom seems to be widespread and unending. But is the world really such a wretched place as this? Is no one happy? Don't the birds sing any more, and are all the flowers in the garden drooping?

Bible readers believe that this is God's world and that he is on the throne. So often however it looks as if the political leaders who can shout the loudest, raise the biggest armies and threaten with the most diabolical weapons really shape our lives. Why can't they use their powers to heal and not to threaten, to relieve distress and not to increase it? There are enough tragedies in life without making more. This is how the writer of Psalm 82 felt. Listen.

How long will you judge unjustly and show partiality to the wicked? Give justice to the weak and the fatherless, maintain the right of the afflicted and the destitute. Rescue the weak and the needy, deliver them from the hand of the wicked. They have neither knowledge nor understanding, they walk about in darkness, all the foundations of the earth are shaken.

And so the cry in which at times we all want to join:

Arise, O God, judge the earth, for to thee belong all the nations!

And he will. God's kingdom will come. Then he will put the wrongs right. This is what his judgment is. Imagine a clock repairer. He doesn't break up the clock brought to him in anger because it is not functioning properly. With patience and care he puts right what is wrong. This is what God will do with his and our world. Only he can put it right.

A prayer

Lord, I grow depressed when I hear only the world's angry voices. Give me grace to believe that you are still on the throne.

You count to God

Her foundations are upon the holy hills: the Lord loveth the gates of Sion more than all the dwellings of Jacob. Very excellent things are spoken of thee: thou city of God. I will think upon Rahab and Babylon: with them that know me. Behold ye the Philistines also: and they of Tyre, with the Morians; lo, there was he born. And of Sion it shall be reported that he was born in her: and the most High shall stablish her. The Lord shall rehearse it when he writeth up the people: that he was born there. The singers also and trumpeters shall he rehearse: All my fresh springs shall be in thee.

This Psalm isn't very easy to make sense of—but it meant a great deal to the writer. He was so bursting with the wonder of the message it contained that he lacked the patience to spell it out. Instead he piled one thought on top of the other—making for something like confusion.

But have you never met someone who has just got back from an exciting experience which they can't wait to tell you about? Breathlessly they pour out their description—but so jumbled that you have to say, 'Just a minute, let us go back to the beginning! What happened first? What came next?' It is a bit like that with this Psalm.

The writer was bursting to say that the time will come when the whole world will acknowledge God as the Sovereign Lord—even those people who are now hostile to the very idea of God. In his day it meant Egypt (Rahab) and Babylon, the great world powers, and the Philistines, Israel's aggressive near neighbours. But in the end race will not count. Whoever will acknowledge God, the Sovereign Lord, God will count as his own. It won't matter where they were born, or if they were complete outsiders.

Hasn't this Psalm got the ring of the Christian gospel about it? 'Whosoever will may come.' 'He that cometh to me I will in no wise cast out.'

A prayer

Lord, I find it hard to believe that you care about me, I am 'small and of no reputation'. But this is the gospel. I will anchor my life there.

Light dispels the darkness

Blessed are the people who know the festal shout, who walk, O Lord, in the light of thy countenance, who exult in thy name all the day, and extol thy righteousness. For thou art the glory of their strength; by thy favour our horn is exulted.

About the end of the first week in January a friend telephoned me. The call was simply for a chat. I was pleased. 'Isn't it lovely,' she said, 'already the evenings are lighter.' I couldn't help smiling to myself because actually at the end of the first week in January there is only an increase in daylight of about 10 minutes or less. But she was happy. She lives in the country and keeps about a dozen cows and a few geese. What was pleasing her was the extra time each day to lock up the animals and do all that has to be done before dark.

Have you noticed that almost the first words in the Bible are about light? 'The earth was without form and void, darkness was upon the face of the deep ... And God said, "Let there be light"; and there was light. And God saw that the light was good; and God separated the light from darkness' (Genesis 1:2–3). The darkness was not capable of stopping what God had intended doing, he *overcame the darkness*, he separated it from the light and then his creative work went forward apace.

Perhaps you are going through a dark patch just now. A few days ago a man heavily engaged in business called on me. We got talking and I realized how hard it was for him to see ahead in the murky world of today's commerce. Your dark patch may be different: health not so good as it was; a family problem; declining income; increased expenditure. Listen to this! God is not overcome by darkness, he separates it out, and light appears, and the work progresses.

The darkness that closed in around the cross on Good Friday did not last. It was real but it was scattered on Easter Sunday morning. The sun streamed into the empty tomb. And before the day was out, the faces of the bewildered disciples were lit up with joy, good to see. It was in the light and the joy of Easter that the Church was born, grew and went forward, proclaiming the light of the world.

Now read the verses again. For 'festal shout' read 'song in the heart'. And when you come to the last verse read the NEB, 'through thy favour we hold our heads high'.

Prayer

Lord, let me hold my head high today, not because I am proud but because I have a song in my heart. I believe the message of Easter—God has banished the darkness, even the darkness of death.

The passing of the years

Teach us to order our days rightly, that we may enter the gate of wisdom.

Turn your hand over. Are there some little brown spots there? And do you forget people's names now? What about going out after dark? Do you mind? If none of this applies don't burden yourself with Psalm 90 now. It is not for you—not yet anyway.

But it is for me, and I will share it with you. The time of life after sixty or after seventy is not however all loss. There are some distinct gains. Passions don't burn as once they did. We can make judgments more objectively. And we don't mind so much what other people think. There is in fact a very real experience of peace.

The hard bit however, the very hard bit, is the loss of people who have made life for us. It feels like an amputation. And of course the more we love the sharper the pain. Yes, I am talking about bereavement and I am not being morbid. Sooner or later we shall, in all probability, have to face it. What then? People will dodge you. And I am tempted to dodge Psalm 90 in the readings. But this would turn me into a fair-weather spiritual guide (if I may dare to call myself that). Bereavement leaves a scar. But there will still be some real joys. This is what Psalm 90 has in mind in the closing verses (read them).

This is as far as the Old Testament can take us, but the New Testament has a ring of certainty about a life beyond death. More than that we believe in the communion of saints. Those we have lost through death are alive to God and praying to him, as we are praying to him, and why not praying for us. Yes we are still together beyond 'the valley of the shadow'. There is life, together, to come.

Prayer

So teach us to number our days: that we may apply our hearts unto wisdom.

Leadership

Moreover, he called for a death upon the land: and destroyed all the provision of bread. But he had sent a man before them: even Joseph, who was sold to be a bond-servant; Whose feet they hurt in the stocks: the iron entered into his soul; Until the time came that his cause was known: the word of the Lord tried him. The king sent, and delivered him: the prince of the people let him go free. He made him lord also of his house: and ruler of all his substance; That he might inform his princes after his will: and teach his senators wisdom.

Every society of people, every community, needs a leader. There cannot be a community holding together without one. But what sort of leader? We have seen some terrible leaders in this century. The word *Führer*, which means leader, still stinks. Our verses today remind us of the type of leader God chooses to acknowledge. The Hebrew people never forgot him any more than they did Abraham, Isaac and Jacob, the forefathers of the nation. They were leaders in faith and obedience to God, but in pastoral situations. Joseph, who followed after, came to leadership on the world stage, controlling the food supplies and therefore the economy and policy of the premier nation of the time, Egypt. However, he began at the bottom of the ladder, even in a place where there was no ladder at all, a foreign prison. They hurt his feet in the stocks there, 'the iron entered his soul'. But he held on to his faith and his integrity.

It is not possible for anyone to lead from any pinnacle of leadership unless he has first learnt how to endure not only hardship but injustice *without resentment.* Not many can achieve this, but leadership requires it because only with this mastery can situations be accurately assessed without personal bias. Before any man or woman sits in any seat of authority he/she must have been *under* authority, the harder the better.

Elitism is out of fashion today, but God has his élite and Joseph was one of them.

A prayer

Lord we pray for our national leaders. May they be strong in faith and integrity.

Lowly people

When I called upon thee, thou heardest me: and enduedst my soul with much strength. All the kings of the earth shall praise thee, O Lord: for they have heard the words of thy mouth. Yea, they shall sing in the ways of the Lord: that great is the glory of the Lord. For though the Lord be high, yet hath he respect unto the lowly: as for the proud he beholdeth them afar off. Though I walk in the midst of trouble, yet shalt thou refresh me: thou shalt stretch forth thy hand upon the furiousness of mine enemies, and thy right hand shall save me. The Lord shall make good his loving-kindness toward me: yea, thy mercy, O Lord, endureth for ever; despise not then the works of thine own hands.

I am sure that Mary the mother of Jesus knew this Psalm. Perhaps she used to sing it to herself. Its message comes out in what we call the Magnificat. 'My soul doth magnify the Lord: and my spirit hath rejoiced in God my Saviour. For he hath regarded the lowliness of his handmaiden.' God does not overlook the lowly people. Nor does he pass by kings and princes if they 'hear the words of God's mouth and sing in the ways of the Lord: that great is the glory of the Lord'. It is the proud and boastful, whether kings or lowly people, whom he passes by till they learn to humble themselves in his presence.

There is another side to this. Because God chooses the 'lowly', the 'lowly' can take a proper estimate of themselves. God chooses to make himself known to people in all walks of life—a few of them 'born with a silver spoon in their mouth', most of them from the most ordinary backgrounds. No one ever needs to write himself or herself off because of a 'lowly' origin. If they are Christians, they can lift up their heads, because God has chosen them—and they can know that he has because God has become real to them. But be careful! It is possible for the 'lowly' to become proud of their faith and then they are 'back at square one'.

A prayer

Lord, I am small and of no reputation—but I will lift up my head, because you have chosen me.

God our protector

I will lift up mine eyes unto the hills: from whence cometh my help. My help cometh even from the Lord: who hath made heaven and earth. He will not suffer thy foot to be moved: and he that keepeth thee will not sleep. Behold, he that keepeth Israel: shall neither slumber nor sleep. The Lord himself is thy keeper: the Lord is thy defence upon thy right hand; So that the sun shall not burn thee by day: neither the moon by night. The Lord shall preserve thee from all evil: yea it is even he that shall keep thy soul. The Lord shall preserve thy going out, and thy coming in: from this time forth for evermore.

When the inhabitants of Jerusalem looked out of their windows, they breathed again. The news being brought into the city was not good. Parts of the surrounding country were being overrun by their enemies. Cities they knew were being occupied. But in Jerusalem they would be safe. How wise King David had been to make this place their capital. The hills all around the city and the rocky precipitous terrain constituted that protection. Jerusalem would be, and was, fortified.

Don't we all think like that sometimes? We shall be all right. We have a good health insurance behind us, a guaranteed pension for when we retire. We have personal skills which will make us useful in our community, a respectable family background, a stainless record in our business life. But even though it is good to have these things they do not constitute our ultimate safety.

This is what Psalm 121 is saying. Perhaps the first verse should be read as a question, 'I will lift up mine eyes unto the hills: from whence doth my help come?' In the last resort it doesn't come from the surrounding precipitous and fortified hills. 'My help cometh even from the Lord who hath made heaven and earth.' Now read the rest of the Psalm. Further comment is unnecessary. It speaks for itself.

A prayer

Lord, sometimes I am complacent when I consider what provision I have made for the future, but at other times I worry about what might happen to me and to the people I love. Help me to hold on to you as my ultimate protector. I am in your hands, and so is everyone whom I love.

Pioneer of salvation

Then he called down a famine on the land: and destroyed the bread that was their stay. But he had sent a man ahead of them: Joseph who was sold into slavery, whose feet they fastened with fetters: and thrust his neck in a hoop of iron. Till the time that his words proved true: he was tested by the Lord's command. Then the king sent and loosed him: the ruler of nations set him free; he made him master of his household: and ruler over all his possessions, to rebuke his officers at will: and to teach his counsellors wisdom.

Yes, I have to grant that 'whose feet they fastened with fetters and thrust his neck into a hoop of iron' is a better translation of the Hebrew than Coverdale's rendering in the Book of Common Prayer, 'whose feet they hurt in the stocks, the iron entered into his soul'. The fetters and the iron hoop are what Joseph had to suffer when he was pulled up out of the pit in which his brothers had thrown him. But 'the iron entered his soul' speaks of the unutterable indignity of it all.

He did not know, of course, that he was being tested. God had great things for him to do. But leaders cannot lead unless they know in experience the meaning of the iron entering the soul. And there was more to come for Joseph. And so it is that the pioneer of our salvation, Christ the Lord, had to taste suffering for everyone. 'For it was fitting that he, for whom and by whom all things exist, in bringing many sons to glory, should make the pioneer of their salvation perfect through suffering' (Hebrews 2:10, RSV).

Prayer

Lord, give me patience in time of adversity. I cannot be what I would be without the experience of pain.

Belonging to God

O Lord you have searched me out and known me: you know when I sit or when I stand you comprehend my thoughts long before. You discern my path and the places where I rest: you are acquainted with all my ways. For there is not a word on my tongue: but you Lord know it altogether... Where shall I go from your spirit: or where shall I flee from your presence? If I ascent into heaven you are there: if I make my bed in the grave you are there also. If I spread out my wings towards the morning: or dwell in the uttermost parts of the sea, even there your hand shall lead me: and your right hand shall hold me.

This Psalm comes from someone sitting in a lonely place, till the conviction is brought home to him that it is impossible to be alone. Wherever you are, God is there before you. And God knows you as no one else can possibly know you— not even the most skilful surgeon equipped with the most up-to-date scanning equipment, and not even the partner of your life who shares in all you do. Only God really knows me. There is nothing in any of the Psalms to come as close as this to the heart of personal religion.

There is no escape from God, and there never will be. At first this sounds frightening, as if God is constantly spying on us. But look at it this way. God will never desert us, for he has made us down to the tiniest bone. He will not toss into the dustbin that on which he has bestowed such creative ingenuity; and there is nothing more wonderful than a human being. To know that we, each one of us, *belongs*, makes all the difference.

A decision

O love that will not let me go, I rest my weary soul on thee.

G. Matheson

Our ultimate security

I lift up my eyes to the hills. From whence does my help come? My help comes from the Lord, who made heaven and earth.

Imagine an inhabitant of Jerusalem (the writer of this Psalm) sitting on one of the hills surrounding the city and taking in the impressive panorama before him. There was the city itself perched on its hill protected by walls. What a sight! And how proud he was of it!

And how envious were the surrounding nations! And how often they made military expeditions to capture it for themselves! And this man, squatting there, began to ask himself what protection the city had from its enemies! Did its security perhaps lie in its extraordinary geographical situation? Jerusalem was not easy to capture. Maybe not, but its ultimate security did not rest in its peculiar location but in God's protection, the God who made heaven and earth. He had chosen Jerusalem.

When you have looked out on your own life with anxiety about the future, have you never answered your own question by telling yourself how well insured you are, how you have a pension scheme, and how there is National Health Security? What is more, you have had a medical check-up and everything seems to be in order. What is there to worry about? Let there be no doubt, all these are a defence against calamity and we need them.

In the last resort, however, God is our real helper. So let us reword the Psalm for our situation:

'I will lift up my eyes to all my securities, insurance policies, and provisions for my future. Does not protection come from these? No, in the last resort it comes from the Lord, my Lord, who has made heaven and earth.'

Something to sing

Glorious things of thee are spoken
Zion, city of our God;
He whose word cannot be broken
Formed thee for his own abode.
On the Rock of ages founded,
What can shake thy sure repose?
With salvation's walls surrounded,
Thou may'st smile at all thy foes.

J. Newton

Joyful laughter

When the Lord turned again the captivity of Sion: then were we like unto them that dream. Then was our mouth filled with laughter: and our tongue with joy. Then said they among the heathen: The Lord hath done great things for them. Yea, the Lord hath done great things for us already: whereof we rejoice.

Picture a great crowd of people in an internment camp. They have been shut in for years. Old people have died there, been buried and mourned. Children have been born there and never known anything else but life behind bars; and prison food and prison beds and prison rules and regulations governing everything anyone wanted to do. No future. The internees had almost forgotten what laughter was like, genuine laughter and not wry laughter.

And then it happened. They could scarcely believe it. Notices plastered up everywhere that on such and such a day the gates would be opened and they would be free. They could go home. Picture the scene. First open-mouthed astonishment. Then disbelief. Gradually belief growing. Then shouting, whistling, dancing and almost uncontrolled laughter. Incredible? Very well, read what happened in the prisoner-of-war camps in Germany at the cessation of hostilities in 1945.

Perhaps it is a 'bit much' to expect us as Christians to laugh and dance and sing like these freed internees, but if we haven't inside us a little merriment on account of our religion we have never reached the heart of the matter; because we have been set free by Christ for time and eternity. That is why he came, to set us free. Do let us have some laughter in our lives in consequence, joyful laughter, grateful laughter.

Thanksgiving

Now thank we all our God,
With heart and hands and voices,
Who wondrous things hath done,
In whom his world rejoices . . .

M. Rinkart

Good days

I give thee thanks, O Lord, with my whole heart; before the gods I sing thy praise; I bow down toward thy holy temple and give thanks to thy name for thy steadfast love and thy faithfulness; for thou hast exalted above everything thy name and thy word. On the day I called, thou didst answer me, my strength of soul thou didst increase. All the kings of the earth shall praise thee, O Lord, for they have heard the words of thy mouth; and they shall sing of the ways of the Lord, for great is the glory of the Lord.

This is one of the good days. Not all days are good days. Sometimes it rains solidly throughout the Bank Holiday just when we had the chance to go out and bask in the sunshine and let the wind blow through our hair. But good days do occur. Some Bank Holidays boast unbroken sunshine. Sometimes all the seeds we sowed come up. Sometimes the holiday place we booked turns out to be a winner. Sometimes what we dearly hopes comes to pass gloriously. What then? Grudging satisfaction? Gloomy forecasts about what will probably happen tomorrow—just as if you know! Take a leaf out of David's Psalm. Let yourself go. Throw yourself into the *joys of the present*. Ladies, put on a new dress. All of you, be as cheerful as you know how. By your demeanour thank God for his goodness *today*. And should this day not turn out to be one of the good, put by this advice for a later day. Wisdom bids us thank God with our whole heart whenever we have half a chance. Few activities are more healthgiving.

Prayer

Lord, the sun is shining today, I see it will be full moon tonight. I feel reasonably well. I have friends who care for me. Underpinning all, I have my faith by virtue of your grace. If I could dance and sing, I would, out of gratitude to you.

All will be well

Hear my prayer, O Lord; give ear to my supplications! In thy faithfulness answer me, in thy righteousness! Enter not into judgment with thy servant; for no man living is righteous before thee. For the enemy has pursued me; he has crushed my life to the ground; he has made me sit in darkness like those long dead. Therefore my spirit faints within me; my heart within me is appalled. I remember the days of old, I meditate on all that thou hast done; I muse on what thy hands have wrought. I stretch out my hands to thee; my soul thirsts for thee like a parched land. Make haste to answer me, O Lord! My spirit fails! Hide not thy face from me, lest I be like those who go down to the Pit. Let me hear in the morning of thy steadfast love, for in thee I put my trust. Teach me the way I should go, for to thee I lift up my soul.

All the way ahead for this writer was dark. In the encircling gloom it was impossible to discern the way ahead, and if perchance there should be turnings to right or left, which to take would be out of the question. There was no hope apart from the guiding hand of God.

But could he rely on this providential leading? Was he worthy of it? Could he possibly expect it? His past was not blameless. But then, whose is? If blamelessness was to be the criterion, then we are all lost.

As he thought about this, musing as it were upon the past, had he not come through many a dark stretch? What more right action then than to appeal to God, to appeal to his loving kindness? And when any one of us casts himself on God trustingly, he will not fail nor forsake us, however unworthy we rightly know ourselves to be.

Prayer

Lead me, Lord, lead me in thy righteousness, make the way plain before my face.

Remember the past

For the enemy has pursued me; he has crushed my life to the ground; he has made me sit in darkness like those long dead. Therefore my spirit faints within me; my heart within me is appalled. I remember the days of old, I meditate on all that thou hast done; I muse on what thy hands have wrought. I stretch out my hands to thee; my soul thirsts for thee like a parched land.

Perhaps you'll think I have an odd mind when I tell you that I see these verses from Psalm 143 as having been written in bed in the early morning. You may know the feeling. You have slept fairly well and now, lying there, you are wide awake. There is a freshness about the new day, and the light streaming in through the window is bright and clear. Yesterday's tiredness has gone, or almost gone. You are about to get up, wash and dress and set about the new day, but you don't—at least, not at once. You lie back and start thinking and (before many minutes have past) worrying. What about that neighbour who has been so difficult? What about that bank overdraft? And Mary's cough doesn't seem to be any better. Can we afford a holiday this year? And the car is showing ominous signs of ageing . . .

If you are no longer young and cannot jump out of bed as you used to, if perhaps you are getting on in years now—and the aches and pains won't let you forget this truth about yourself— you have one advantage over the young. You have a past to remember, events that still stand out in your mind on which you can meditate. You came through those tough patches, and you didn't go under. You believed God was your deliverer. And so lying there on your bed in the early morning you stretch, as it were, your hands out to God, asking him to see you through the coming day as he has led you through all the days in the past.

Don't forget the past and what God has done for you. He will do it again if you trust him. So rise up from your bed and put a good face on the new day.

A prayer

Lord, I remember that day, and that other day, and that whole week. It was a terrible week; but you saw me through it all. I trust you to do it again.

Happiness

Save me, and deliver me from the hand of strange children; whose mouth talketh of vanity, and their right hand is a right hand of iniquity. That our sons may grow up as the young plants: and that our daughters may be as the polished corners of the temple. That our garners may be full and plenteous with all manner of store: that our sheep may bring forth thousands and ten thousands in our streets. That our oxen may be strong to labour, that there be no decay: no leading into captivity, and no complaining in our streets. Happy are the people that are in such a case: yea, blessed are the people who have the Lord for their God.

I am afraid you've got it wrong, David, if it was you who wrote this Psalm. I see it is really a prayer, and there is no harm in your praying it even if it is wrong because God will quickly cross out what is inappropriate. God does this with our prayers, which is one reason why we can pray freely. But look! There is nothing wrong with wanting strong sons, beautiful daughters, barns chock full of grain, sheep and cattle breeding young, and no diseases; better still an absence of war and the whole community satisfied—marvellous! But if you think the possession of them is going to bring you happiness I'm afraid you've got it all wrong. I'm told that if you really want to see bored faces (as if anyone would!) you should book in to one of those super luxury cruises in the Caribbean. Happiness stems from inside people, not from luxuries outside.

I read about a class of ten-year-old girls talking about their future. And didn't they talk! One wanted to be a television announcer, another a circus director, another an interpreter. The girl sitting next to her was silent. Was she still thinking about it? No, she was quite clear what she wanted to be. And when the teacher asked her for her answer she replied, 'I would like to be happy.' Everyone was astonished. They didn't know what to say. But she was right. Happiness is more important than possessions or position and they do not provide it automatically. The root of happiness is to know that you are safe in the hands of God come what may.

A prayer

Thank you, Lord, for the good things in my life, more than some people have, less than others: but enough to know that you have provided for me and will never forsake me.

Our ultimate security

Praise the Lord, O my soul; while I live I praise the Lord: yea, as long as I have any being, I will sing praises unto my God. O put not your trust in princes, nor in any child of man: for there is no help in them. For when the breath of man goeth forth he shall turn again to his earth: and then all his thoughts perish.

Whoever wrote this Psalm— perhaps it was David, we don't know—must have tasted more than once the bitter gall of being let down by someone, or some group of people, whom he thought he could trust. Perhaps a political leader, perhaps 'a friend in high places', perhaps some fortune-teller who promised great things, perhaps a new party of reform, perhaps a cute business deal. And of course he becomes disillusioned, possibly a trifle cynical, certainly pretty 'canny' in future. Anyone who thinks everything in the garden is going to be lovely because of what people promise is either very young or a fool.

The stark truth is—all men's and women's powers, however impressive, are failing powers. They are on the way to ceasing altogether. There is no permanent application in them. They are not made of the stuff of eternity. Why? Read verse 3 again.

But are we left then hopeless and helpless, driftwood on the shores of time? No we are not. There is a God, the Eternal God, the undying God, made known supremely in Jesus of Nazareth, the Risen Christ. This is where our trust is secure, only here.

Sing, then! I don't know about lifting up our voice till the final breath (verse 1). That is a bit much, but as long as we can. (Always, everywhere, we can 'lift up our hearts'.)

And don't forget Paul and Silas sang *in prison* (Acts 16:25).

Our caring God

Blessed is he that hath the God of Jacob for his help: and whose hope is in the Lord his god; Who made heaven and earth, the sea, and all that therein is: who keepeth his promise for ever; Who helpeth them to right that suffer wrong; who feedeth the hungry. The Lord looseth men out of prison: the Lord giveth sight to the blind. The Lord helpeth them that are fallen: the Lord careth for the righteous. The Lord careth for the strangers; he defendeth the fatherless and widow: as for the way of the ungodly, he turneth it upside down.

Think of the sky, the earth, the sea, the changing seasons, seedtime and harvest. We can rely on them. They won't suddenly alter their ways. And God made them. God is shown thereby to be trustworthy. He won't let us down as people so often do.

And the reason? Unlike humankind God is not self-centred. He is not concerned with his own welfare. Nor does he 'look over his shoulder' at the well-heeled and influential only, those who are privileged and successful. He also 'helpeth them to right that suffer wrong: who feedeth the hungry'. And he notes in particular the lonely. Typical are those in prison, not necessarily in gaols, but prisoner to a disabled body, a broken home, a boring job. And men and women limited and isolated by blindness. And people who have made a mess of their lives or acted foolishly. (Is this why verse 4 speaks of the God *of Jacob*— the 'twister' whom God helped so greatly?) And outsiders. And 'latch key' children. The God whom we can trust cares.

Don't dodge the second half of verse 9. If God were not a God of judgment, he would be immoral.

If you can still sing, have a go at the last verse of the '*Te Deum*'. I am doing so now (Stanford in B flat!). 'O Lord, in thee have I trusted: let me never be confounded.'

The meek

Great is our Lord, and great is his power: yea, and his wisdom is infinite. The Lord setteth up the meek: and bringeth the ungodly down to the ground.

I don't know where the Psalmist got this idea from! Looking around him he must have seen how 'the weakest go to the wall', and how the prizes of life apparently go to the thrusters, the 'go-getters' and the pot-hunters. If you don't stick up for yourself, no one else will. This is the general philosophy of life. Read the books of Samuel in the Old Testament. It always has been so.

But maybe we are mistaken about meekness. A meek person is not one who can't say 'boo' to a goose, or is obsequiously 'umble like Uriah Heep. There is little attraction in such types, and they do not accomplish much in life. No, a meek man or woman is one who sees himself/herself as in the hands of God. Such a person may rise to the top, become a leader, command enormous respect, and at whatever the level of achievement publicly, or privately, gets things done. But he does not put all this down to his own strength. He sincerely believes himself to be God's instrument, although he does not talk about it.

How else would you account for *Moses* being described in the Bible as a meek man? Is it conceivable that he could have led a rabble of Hebrew slaves out of slavery in Egypt to weld them into a nation had he been a 'pussy-footed' individual? Moses was a giant of a man.

But the world had to wait a long time to see real meekness. This was in Jesus of Nazareth. Did he sit down under the Pharisees' trumped-up conviction? *But he trusted God wholly.* That was his meekness. Therefore God set him up and brought down to the ground those who set him at nought. It is not they whom we honour today. God's wisdom is infinite. The proud fall, not the meek.

A prayer

Lord, I am what I am, and can do what I can do, through your grace alone.

Sad days and sad songs

Is there anyone who knows nothing of sad days? And you can't always throw them off. Some cut far too deep for that. And mingling in a jolly party will not help, when the time comes to go home the heartache is worse. Sometimes we only have ourselves to blame. But more often than not the calamity, the loss, the let-down, the illness will not go away, it has just hit us.

How does the Psalmist handle situations like this? How does the artist handle them—the painter, the composer, the poet? Does he or she deliberately avoid them? Does he say that he doesn't want to make people miserable? He will be no great artist, composer or poet if he does. So because he has stature in him, sensitivity and depth of character, understanding life and people, he will be sparing of gaudy pictures, jolly tunes able to be whistled on the way home, and verses that require no concentrated attention.

Certainly light approaches have their place, but if he is to take hold of people there will have to be dark patches and sad, solemn melodies. Why? Because life is like that at times, and to mirror life they must be included.

Have you never seen an audience in a concert hall spellbound by music so melancholy you could cry over it? Don't be surprised then that the Psalmist does not play simple tinkly tunes in his manuscript but some that are solemn, sombre and sad. What he is doing is introducing God in those situations and this gives his work its distinctive and rare quality.

Prayer

Lord, I doubt if the sun will shine in my heart today, even if it streams down out there in the park. I miss those I love no longer with us, I have to see the doctor and am worried what his verdict may be, I am wondering how to make ends meet financially, I have this awful pain in my back which won't go away. Lord, I am not hiding my troubles from you. You know about pain and grief. You know about clouds and darkness, and if I tried to keep all my sadness to myself I should only increase my sorrows. So Lord I tell you my sorry story, I lay before you all that is 'getting me down', I acknowledge my weakness, I would only do this to my best friend who understands me, but that is what you are to me, and far more.

Up against it

O Lord, how many are my foes! Many are rising against me; many are saying of me, there is no help for him in God. But thou, O Lord, art a shield about me, my glory and the lifter of my head. I cry aloud to the Lord, and he answers me from his holy hill. I lie down and sleep; I wake again, for the Lord sustains me. I am not afraid of ten thousands of people who have set themselves against me round about.

Whoever composed this Psalm and in what circumstances we don't know but clearly it was someone in a desperate situation. Perhaps he was a survivor from a bloody battle creeping into hiding places to save his very life, appalled at the number of people out to catch him and finish him off. He felt they were crouching behind every rock, hidden in every bush, ready to pounce. And those attackers were confident that nothing could save this escapee, certainly not his religious faith for which they had no use whatsoever. In other words he was a man who hadn't a chance. But he, for his part, did not despair, he did not abandon hope. He called on God to shield him, and was confident that his prayer would be answered. Most striking of all, he slept at nights, and it was as well he did because without sleep he would never hold out. He felt that God was sustaining him for some good purpose. So, many against one, that is the picture. No, not exactly, it was many against one plus God, and that plus made all the difference.

Many of us, perhaps all of us, have times when we are up against it in life. Troubles and problems crowd upon us. They seem to be around every corner. We are desperate. We all but lose our heads. The mortgage arrears, the threat of redundancy, health problems. What next? Oh yes, the children have failed their examinations at school. Troubles on all sides. If people mock us for our church-going—'Fat lot of good that does them' they say—it is not surprising if we feel bitterly hurt in such circumstances.

And then we are reminded of someone who experienced similar circumstances and came through, and for us today in our reading that someone is the Psalmist. He turned to God for help, he even slept at nights without waking at four a.m. God was his shield.

Prayer

Lord, when I am trapped by circumstances show me the way out and give me a quiet mind.

'Browned off'

There are many who say. 'O that we might see some good! Lift up the light of thy countenance upon us, O Lord!' Thou hast put more joy in my heart than they have when their grain and wine abound. In peace I will both lie down and sleep; for thou alone, O Lord, makest me dwell in safety.

'Browned off'. We are experiencing this nationwide at the present time. Distrustful of our political leaders who seem chiefly bent on scoring points off each other, we have grown too bored to listen. Half the population can't be bothered to vote at elections. We doubt if anything will be accomplished whichever way we vote. There is very little to uplift our hearts. No doubt it is entirely wrong to slide into the slough of despond but the reasons are clear. We have waited a long time for better times to come, and they haven't, except for a tiny few. And, where conditions have eased, money speedily becomes the be-all and end-all of their lives. And this materialism compounds to keep down dissatisfaction with life itself. People get 'browned off'.

'Browned off' people make poor companions. They can't get going with anything very much. 'What is the use?' is their stock phrase. And they inhibit us all by being so disillusioned.

There is only one remedy for this situation. It is to believe that God has the situation in control, and that means your situation, my situation and the world's situation. We need to 'let go and let God'. This is no easy option, but apparently the writer of this Psalm achieved it. Read the closing verses. He could even sleep at night and no doubt woke up refreshed. He was convinced that God alone makes us dwell in safety, not least from the peril of disillusionment, or to use the slang phrase 'being browned off'.

Prayer

Lord, I confess that sometimes I fall into the slough of despond, and I ought not to. Make yourself known to me, so that I may lift up my head.

Down the drain

O Lord, rebuke me not in thy anger, nor chasten me in thy wrath. Be gracious to me, O Lord, for I am languishing; O Lord, heal me, for my bones are troubled. My soul also is sorely troubled. But thou, O Lord—how long? Turn, O Lord, save my life; deliver me for the sake of thy steadfast love. For in death there is no remembrance of thee; in Sheol who can give thee praise?

Have you ever been down the drain with a most unbearable pain till you cried out for mercy? If not, you don't know the full extent of human existence. But the Psalmist knew. He has written from experience. You can't pray, you can't think of anyone but yourself, the pain won't let you. If you pray at all it will be nothing more than 'Lord, have mercy'. And if someone who really loves you comes to sit by your bedside, he or she doesn't talk, only holds your hand very gently with an occasional squeeze to let you know that you are not alone. And you go on stuffing the corners of the sheet in your mouth and biting them hard. Not even tears will come.

Was the Psalmist partly responsible for what had overtaken him? Possibly (see verse 1). Is this why his soul was in anguish? (verse 3). And maybe he had lapsed into thinking that his pain was God's punishment for something he had done wrong. But God dosen't act like that. When we are down the drain he is not angry but desperately sorry. This is why we can cry to him for help (verse 4). Note the words 'unfailing love'. But the pain doesn't cease all at once and not surprisingly the sufferer makes some random remarks which bear little wisdom

or even sense, but don't lay blame on a man when in terrible pain. I suggest verse 5 be read in this light: 'For in death there is no remembrance of thee; in Sheol who can give thee praise?' Of course not, but his pain is so great, he thinks he must be going to die.

But he turns the corner and recovers, convinced that God has heard his prayer. People are astounded at his recovery and some even ashamed of their confident predictions of his death (see verse 10). They wanted him out of the way. But the sufferer knew why he was suffering and the knowledge multiplied his misery. All that is now behind him and as a result of his experience he will be a more mature person, painful though it was. Perhaps we cannot be mature Christians till we know what it is like to be down the drain and to come up again.

Prayer

Lord, I look back on those days of unbearable pain, but you sustained me and here I am to praise your name.

An appeal

O Lord my God, in thee do I take refuge; save me from all my pursuers, and deliver me, lest like a lion they rend me, dragging me away with none to rescue. O Lord my God, if I have done this, if there is wrong in my hands, if I have requited my friends with evil or plundered my enemy without cause, let the enemy pursue me and overtake me, and let him trample my life to the ground and lay my soul in the dust. Arise, O Lord, in thy anger, lift thyself up against the fury of my enemies, awake O my God; thou hast appointed a judgment.

Psalm after Psalm which we read shows David in a sticky patch, many sticky patches. Someone is always pursuing him, determined to kill, and mostly at King Saul's instigation, for he saw David as his rival to the throne. Note then how these early Psalms in the Psalter arose out of situations of travail. But isn't this true to life? The lilies entrancing us on the still waters of the pond grow out of the sludge and muck in the bottom. And aren't some of the most moving of Beethoven's symphonies and piano concertos those which are threaded with sadness? No, don't write off the tough periods of your life, they can be the most creative.

Two other points. David protested his innocence of deliberate wrong-doing. Ought he? But if we mustn't make out that we are better than we are, neither must we make out that we are worse than we are. Be honest. Be honest with God.

Note how David asked for God's protection. He would not take *all* matters into his own hands.

Prayer

Lord, teach me how to make every setback an opportunity.

Hope in gloom

Help, Lord; for there is no longer any that is godly; for the faithful have vanished from among the sons of men. Every one utters lies to his neighbour: with flattering lips and a double heart they speak. May the Lord cut off all flattering lips, the tongue that makes great boasts, those who say, 'With our tongue we will prevail, our lips are with us; who is our master?' 'Because the poor are despoiled, because the needy groan, I will now arise,' says the Lord; 'I will place him in the safety for which he longs.' The promises of the Lord are promises that are pure, silver refined in a furnace on the ground, purified seven times. Do thou, O Lord, protect us, guard us ever from this generation. On every side the wicked prowl, as vileness is exalted among the sons of men.

We prefer happy, joyful songs. This is understandable, but life isn't all jolly, and if our Christian worship doesn't sometimes touch us at the sombre points with a message it is failing. This Psalm is a complaint but it does manage to rise above the gloom once or twice and confidence takes hold.

What is the trouble? It is the decadence that has crept in among God's people. Perhaps this Psalm was written when David's kingdom was established and the temple worship was splendid with entrancing music supported by professional singers. On the surface then everything was splendid but underneath the beautiful and orderly façade—'Everyone utters lies to his neighbour; with flattering lips and a double heart they speak.' The state religion has grown corrupt. Nothing was what it seemed.

And yet it could not be wholly corrupt because some worshippers were aware of that corruption. There was still a faithful remnant and if there was hope anywhere, it lay with this minority. They heard God's voice and they believed his promises made and purified in times of affliction. And they prayed to God to protect them from the generation which was acting so vilely.

This is a picture of Church decadence. Does it in any way relate to us? Read, if you have the nerve, the history of the Christian Church—a sorry story of a Church corrupted too often by power. At the heart of the corruption is what is said with the lips and what is actually carried out. They do not tally, so truth falls to the ground and the faithful are scarcely to be found any more (verse 1).

Yes, a sad Psalm, but God will turn our heaviness into joy.

Prayer

Lord, let us not lose our hope. In your good time the truth will be established.

Down at the bottom

My God, my God, why hast thou forsaken me and art so far from saving me, from heeding my groans? O my God, I cry in the day-time but thou dost not answer, in the night I cry but get no respite. And yet thou art enthroned in holiness, thou art he whose praises Israel sings. In thee our fathers put their trust; they trusted, and thou didst rescue them. Unto thee they cried and were delivered; in thee they trusted and were not put to shame. But I am a worm, not a man, abused by all men, scorned by the people.

Do we have to read these depressing verse? Can't we tear them out of the Bible leaving only the inspiring bits? Who wants to be made miserable? If, however, we did this, the scriptures would only speak to part of our experience, because at times we are wretched like the writer of these verses. George Orwell wasn't far out when he wrote, 'Most people get a fair amount of fun out of their lives, but on balance life is suffering, and only the very young or the very foolish imagine otherwise'.

Physical pain is the trouble here, the kind of pain which for its intensity and duration scorches you. Some will know what this like. You can't think of anything or anybody. You certainly can't pray. There is nothing but the pain. The whole world has shrunk to that one thing. You are down at the bottom.

Please God you who read this won't descend there today, but if you do, remember this—others have been down there before you, and among them, chiefest among them, Jesus Christ our Lord. Don't we say in the Creed, 'He descended into Hell'? But God brought him out didn't he? He does not fail nor forsake us.

Pray today

For any known to be ill, the broken in body, some broken in mind, the blind, the deaf, the crippled; Lord, have mercy upon them, I beseech you.

Caught in a net

My eyes are ever looking to the Lord: for he will bring my feet out of the net. Turn your face toward me and be gracious, for I am alone and in misery. O free my heart from pain: and bring me out of my distress. Give heed to my affliction and adversity: and forgive me all my sins. Consider my enemies how many they are, and they bear a violent hate against me. O keep by me and deliver me: put me not to shame for I come to you for refuge.

In May I spread a nylon net over my gooseberry bushes. I haven't many, only three, and I did not see why the birds should eat the modest crop I hoped to gather from them. After all, I had done all the work. Pruning, digging around and spraying. But a blackbird got caught in the net. A fine specimen with a lovely yellow beak. He struggled this way and that, but his wings were hopelessly entangled and so were his legs. He was frantic. Of course he resisted my help, but I did succeed in setting him free. I wish I could say that he flew up into a tree and sang a little song to thank me. But he didn't, and I didn't expect it . . .

Many people, alas, feel netted in life. Perhaps their job is restrictive. Perhaps they suffer from some disability. Perhaps they are held back by a poor education. Perhaps they are short of money and the mortgage payments are a continual worry. Some, sad to say, feel netted by their family. They can't get free. This is the trouble for all netted people.

Read the Psalm again and you will see how it fits.

We may not be able to be set free from our restrictions. An obvious case is the limitations that come with advancing years, and there are others. But we can be set free from the resentment which too often is the accompaniment and need not be. It is always possible to have a *free spirit*. Let us not forget that Christ set us free from our nets.

A prayer

Lord, from the nets of resentment, jealousy, hatred and all bad habits, I pray thee to set me free.

Dig deeper

When the righteous cry for help, the Lord hears, and delivers them out of all their troubles. The Lord is near to the broken-hearted, and saves the crushed in spirit. Many are the afflictions of the righteous; but the Lord delivers him out of them all. He keeps all his bones; Not one of them is broken. Evil shall slay the wicked; and those who hate the righteous will be condemned. The Lord redeems the life of his servants; none of those who take refuge in him will be condemned.

O dear! Isn't it a bit simplistic? What about Auschwitz? What about Christ himself? Did God deliver him from the tortures of that wooden cross with nails to keep him there? And haven't we seen some ungodly 'get away with' their evil doings? So David you will have to dig a little deeper than rest with a simple theology of God delivering the good from all their troubles and bringing desolation on the ungodly! There is such a thing as God delivering us *through* suffering. I won't say *sending* us suffering to remake us, but using the 'changes and chances of this mortal life' to occasion us a rise in faith so that we hold on. Then we are being delivered from the smallness of our natural selves into beings with at least some vestige of stature. With faith in God we are made *through suffering.* Those who rebel in unfaith break themselves down.

Prayer

Lord, I am like most people, I shrink from pain, I dread adversity, I doubt how I shall stand up when trouble comes to knock at my door. Lord, show me how to react positively, how to see opportunities in apparent limitations and above all to hold close to you.

Melancholy

I held my tongue, and spake nothing: I kept silence, yea, even from good words; but it was pain and grief to me. My heart was hot within me, and while I was thus musing the fire kindled: and at the last I spake with my tongue. Lord, let me know mine end, and the number of my days: that I may be certified how long I have to live. Behold, thou hast made my days as it were a span long: and mine age is even as nothing in respect of thee; and verily every man living is altogether vanity. For man walketh in a vain shadow, and disquieteth himself in vain: he heapeth up riches, and cannot tell who shall gather them. And now, Lord, what is my hope: truly my hope is even in thee.

Many of these early Psalms have roots in the youthful and turbulent period of David's life. But life does not continue in this frenzied activity; it calms down.

Then we perhaps start thinking. We have time to think—maybe cannot for a time anyway do much else but think. We get stuck in a hospital bed, as I am now yet again, as I write this. Perhaps David growing older was forced to reset limbs wounded from his military campaigning youth, nursing also his inner misgivings. What was the worth of all that struggling activity? The question forced itself across his lips. And what final profit to those wearing themselves out to amass money? And so the writer inspired the phrase which haunts me for the sheer beauty of its language in the Prayer Book version: 'For man walketh in a vain shadow, and disquieteth himself in vain.' But he came out of his melancholy into a proper faith. 'And now Lord, what is my hope: truly my hope is even in thee.' Wonderful!

Pray

for any elderly people you know who have not found the secret of how to struggle out of melancholy.

Catastrophes

God is our hope and strength: a very present help in trouble. Therefore will we not fear, though the earth be moved: and though the hills be carried into the midst of the sea.

What is in mind here is troubles on a *world scale*. And we cannot dodge them. This is the terror of television. It brings murder and rape and hunger and devastation from earthquake, famine and flood right into our sitting-rooms at the end of the day, just when we are relaxing after the day's work. But we can't relax. It gets us 'worked up'. And people who live alone say, 'It gets you down.' And no small part of the trouble is caused by the fact that we can do very little about these world catastrophes, beyond responding possibly to an appeal for financial help from some relief fund.

We aren't wrong to be upset. We would be callous creatures if we were not; but the tragedy is that if we hear too much and too long of nothing but calamities we become insensitive to them. The human heart does not possess the capacity to take on the troubles of the world. So what should we do? Switch off the television? Stop taking a daily newspaper? This may be the right action sometimes but it is too negative to deal with our fears. We shall know all the time that the catastrophes are continuing.

We must bring God into our picture of the world. It is, after all, his world, not mine or yours. Actually I am his too and so are you. Some people will say, 'Ah! But it is because of these catastrophes that we cannot believe in God any more.' But are catastrophes new? Were there no catastrophes in the Psalmist's day when he wrote the verse we have just read? Read our Old Testament. Plenty of carnage and cruelty there. But 'God is our hope and strength...'

A prayer

Lord, sometimes I get 'worked up' about air pollution, about the spoilation of the environment, the terrorism, the vandalism and the burglars. I can't help it. I am made that way. Lord, let me see you in control. I want to be a strong person. You can make me strong.

Hiding among the enemy

Be gracious to me, O God, for men trample upon me; all day long foemen oppress me; my enemies trample upon me all day long, for many fight against me proudly. When I am afraid, I put my trust in thee. In God, whose word I praise, in God I trust without a fear. What can flesh do to me? All day long they seek to injure my cause; all their thoughts are against me for evil. They band themselves together, they lurk, they watch my steps. As they have waited for my life . . .

David was desperate where to go after he had run from Ahimelech, the Priest of Nob, with the sword of Goliath of Gath in his hand. Saul's soldiers were poking into every Judaean cave to catch him. No place seemed safe. But what about hiding among Saul's enemies, the Philistines? What about Achish, the king of Seth way out west on the Judaean Philistine frontier? Achish wasn't totally unfriendly. So he went. But did his subtle plan work? It did not. Achish's servant whispered, 'Is not this David the *king* of the land?' Did they not sing one to another of him in dances saying, 'Saul hath slain his thousands, but David his ten thousands'? Fear for his life gripped David's heart. What escape route remained now? One idea, a crazy one, but he snatched at it. He feigned madness and clawed at the doors of the gate. Achish had no time for madmen, he turned him out.

We want to close the book. What can such violent escapades say to us? But what man or woman of faith, what Christian, has not at some time sought to lie low about his faith in some reli-giously hostile community and keep his/her mouth shut? Poor David, poor you, poor me, when we find ourselves in an alien community. Now read the Psalm again.

Prayer

Save me, O Lord, when I am desperately alone.

Encirclement

Deliver me from my enemies, O my God, protect me from those who rise up against me, deliver me from those who work evil, and save me from bloodthirsty men. For, lo, they lie in wait for my life; fierce men band themselves against me. For no transgression or sin of mine, O Lord, for no fault of mine, they run and make ready. Rouse thyself, come to my help, and see! Thou, Lord God of hosts, art God of Israel. Awake to punish all the nations; spare none of those who treacherously plot evil.

Saul, the once impressive first king of Israel, became so consumed with jealousy of David the shepherd-lad whom he brought into his royal court that his mind became warped. The tragedy was that David attracted Saul—his looks, his musical and poetic gifts, the cunning of his fingers and his astonishing prowess in the martial arts. What a king David would make! How the people would come flocking to this young 'wonder man'. And then Saul's countenance darkened. His eyes burned fiercely. David was becoming his rival in the kingdom. How long would it be before David supplanted him? He, Saul, must strike first.

Now David had his eye on Saul's flashy daughter, Michal, but he, a shepherd's son, could never hope to aspire to a royal marriage. Michal, for her part, was fascinated by David. Saul saw his chance. He gave his daughter to David in marriage. It would enrage the Philistines and they would seek to kill David. Desperate because this ruse failed, he sent soldiers to encircle David and Michal's house, waiting to strike the fatal blow. But it didn't work. Michal deceived them and David made his getaway.

Now read the Psalm again. Can you, can I, put ourselves in David's shoes?

Prayer

Lord, I have never been in such a plight as this but I believe you are round about my life to save me.

In the deep

Save me, O God: for the waters are come in, even unto my soul. I stick fast in the deep mire, where no ground is: I am come into deep waters, so that the floods run over me ... Hear me, O God, in the multitude of thy mercy: even in the truth of thy salvation. Take me out of the mire, that I sink not: O let me be delivered from them that hate me, and out of the deep waters. Let not the water-flood drown me, neither let the deep swallow me up: and let not the pit shut her mouth upon me.

I would not recognize you as someone I could understand if you told me you had never been in the deep like the writer of the above prayer for deliverance, because that is what it is. Have you never been let down by a friend and cried your heart out? Do you know nothing of that empty feeling when you walk away from a hospital ward knowing that there can't be many more visits, for that patient's illness is incurable; it is only a matter of time? Or you are short of money. Or your job is likely to come to an end. Or you wonder how you will 'cope' when you are old. Or you have made an awful blunder and can't see how you can escape the consequence.

If you don't know life turning this kind of face towards you, ugly and menacing, then you had better tear up Psalm 69, it has nothing for you. But Jesus knew it. He sank in the deep mire where no ground is, and he prayed this Psalm. So keep it by you. You may need it some day.

A prayer

Lord, remember today the broken-hearted, the faint-hearted, and all those who have completely lost heart: Thou, Lord, unto whom all hearts are open, all desires known, Lift them up I beseech thee, and let them praise thy name.

Life's rough patches

Blessed is the man whose strength is in thee: in whose heart are thy ways. Who going through the vale of misery use it for a well: and the pools are filled with water. They will go from strength to strength: and unto the God of gods appeareth every one of them in Sion. O Lord God of hosts, hear my prayer: hearken, O God of Jacob.

Perhaps someone reading this note is quite young. If so, you will have been before some sort of selection board. Perhaps it was a job interview—and you can get a bit worried. 'What shall I wear?' 'How much shall I tell them about myself?' 'What are my ambitions?' And perhaps you think, 'It's all right for the interviewers. I wouldn't mind being in their shoes!' And now some years have rolled away and you are in their position. You are on a board of management and have to choose between twenty or thirty candidates for a job. It is a tough assignment and it carries responsibilities. It requires skills and personality to make a success of it. And suppose the wrong candidate is chosen from among the applicants. The selectors will bear much of the blame for the consequent failures. It isn't only the interviewees who dread the selection day. So do the interviewers!

How can we tell if that person will make a success of the job? We can't ever be sure. But we would be well-advised to avoid the candidate for whom everything has come on a plate. We would do better to concentrate on the one or two who have battled through difficul-

ties, who have known the taste of hardship and disappointment, and who instead of going under or reacting bitterly have used those rough patches to acquire added strength. If that person has achieved this trusting in the good hand of God on their life then that is probably the candidate to choose. They will go from strength to strength, and they won't let us down.

A prayer

Lord, I dare to thank you for the rough patches in my life. Give me wisdom to draw strength from them.

The deserts of life

Blessed are the men whose strength is in thee, in whose heart are the highways to Zion. As they go through the valley of Baca they make it a place of springs; the early rain also covers it with pools. They go from strength to strength; the God of gods will be seen in Zion.

Now be honest! These verses might as well be written in double Dutch for all the sense they make to most of you; and let me be honest, for all they meant to me for a very long time.

Let me spell this out. Here are some pilgrims on the way to Jerusalem. They know how rough the going will be. They will have to go through the valley of Baca where there isn't a drop of water. It is an absolute desert, but they keep their destination in mind all the rough way—beautiful, beautiful Zion, and it sustains them. Their thoughts turn the dry valley into a place of springs, making them even stronger than they would normally be; indeed, they go from strength to strength because they know the God of gods will be seen in Zion at their journey's end.

The other day I read about a man who went to visit his mother in hospital. Every day she was growing weaker. Putting his arm around her shoulder he eased her up so that she could sip the weak cup of tea he was holding for her. She struggled, but wasn't very successful. Then, trying hard to fix her eyes, she looked him straight in the face and whispered. 'Goodbye, John.' And those were the last two words she spoke. The son then broke down, sobbing. His wife, also present, had seen him once in his life shed a tear or two, but nothing like this. He was crumpled up with grief, a broken man, almost a stranger. She wondered what life would be like with him in the future. They got on reasonably well in their married life but there was no real closeness in mind and spirit. His male reserve had been a barrier, and that breaking down by the bedside turned out to be a blessing. The wife need not have dreaded the future, for the desert had become a place of springs.

This is a lesson. With our trust fixed in God we can draw refreshment from the arid stretches of life, and in consequence become stronger people. We must not write off the deserts, for we can make them pools of water.

A prayer

Lord, help me face the troubles of this present day, with my eyes fixed on your care and concern. Let them be like pools of water in the desert for me.

Crying

Incline thy ear, O Lord, and answer me, for I am poor and needy. Preserve my life, for I am godly; save thy servant who trusts in thee. Thou art my God; be gracious to me, O Lord, for to thee do I cry all the day. Gladden the soul of thy servant, for to thee, O Lord, do I lift up my soul. For thou, O Lord art good and forgiving, abounding in steadfast love to all who call on thee. Give ear, O Lord to my prayer; hearken to my cry of supplication. In the day of my trouble I call on thee, for thou dost answer me.

There does not exist any even flimsy ground for attaching this Psalm to any *particular* incident in David's life. Clearly, however, the writer was weary with the very 'on and on-ness' of his reversals of fortune. Every day brought stress, great stress. But his faith in God's rescuing mercies never deserted him. I see him dragging himself from his miserable couch morning after morning wondering if he can endure the struggle another day. And then he remembered God, the God in whom he trusted. The God who is good and gracious and of great mercy to them that call upon him. This put new heart into him, and the courage to struggle on. He would call daily upon God.

Are we wearied by the undoubted fact that so many of these Psalms are plaintive and stem from the bitter struggles of the early part of David's life before he obtained the throne? But I think of this: deep spiritual experiences rarely arise out of 'the plain sailing' patches of life, nor does the poetry, nor does the music where deep calls unto deep. So do not respond only to the hallelujahs in the Psalms, learn too from the crying.

Prayer

Lord, I have cried. Perhaps I should not be what I am today, had I not cried. I know now that you hear us when we cry.

154

God as shelter

He who dwells in the shelter of the Most High: who abides under the shadow of the Almighty, he will say to the Lord, 'You are my refuge and my stronghold: my God in whom I trust.' For he will deliver you from the snare of the hunter: and from the destroying curse. He will cover you with his wings and you will be safe under his feathers: his faithfulness will be your shield and defence. You shall not be afraid of any terror by night: or of the arrow that flies by day, of the pestilence that walks about in darkness: or the plague that destroys at noonday.

Each stage of life has its own particular perils. At each of these stages wisdom counsels that we have God as a refuge.

At twenty we have to be on our guard against recklessness. It is a fine thing to possess energy, thrust and strong emotional responses. Life is there to be enjoyed to the full. We are scarcely aware of limitations. We can do what we want to do, and we will 'jolly well' do it! The enemy then is recklessness, ready to take over and spoil everything. Think, man! Think, woman! Think! God has made wisdom a refuge. Keep it in regard.

At forty there are two contrary enemies to successful living. One is laziness: 'I've done it all now, I can sit back.' The other is preoccupation with the busyness of 'getting on', and such overloading of responsibilities that there is no time for worship. Then we need a refuge from materialism. We must run for shelter in God.

At sixty we begin to know the meaning of limitations. We can't do what we once did. And bereavement sooner or later becomes a hurting reality. The love of God is needed then as a refuge from anxiety. God will provide.

The storms of life

They that go down to the sea in ships: and occupy their business in great waters; These men see the works of the Lord: and his wonders in the deep. For at his word the stormy wind ariseth: which lifteth up the waves thereof. They are carried up to the heaven, and down again to the deep: their soul melteth away because of the trouble. They reel to and fro, and stagger like a drunken man: and are at their wits' end. So when they cry unto the Lord in their trouble: he delivereth them out of their distress. For he maketh the storm to cease: so that the waves thereof are still. Then are they glad, because they are at rest: and so he bringeth them unto the haven where they would be. O that men would therefore praise the Lord for his goodness: and declare the wonders that he doeth for the children of men!

Last week I read about a retired couple suddenly hit by one of the storms of life driving them almost to their wits' end. The husband suffered severely with arthritis, making movement around the house a painful business. He needed constant help from his wife, who was feeling her age. One fateful day she slipped and broke her leg. Complications set in; she became confined to her bed. Where they lived social service was non-existent. There was nothing for it but for the old man to nurse and care for his wife himself. This he did with never failing patience for two whole years till she died. How he found the strength for this will never be known, but he did. Life isn't all plain sailing. Storms blow up and we only just manage to reach our harbour and that at considerable cost. We don't drown, however. We pull through. And how thankful we are.

How shall I manage if . . .? Let today's Psalm remind us that sometimes God makes the storms to cease, and if this does not happen gives us the strength to weather them.

A prayer

Lord, I wondered if I would pull through but I did pull through. I don't know how, but you know. You do not fail nor forsake us.

Down in the depths

I cried unto the Lord with my voice: yea, even unto the Lord did I make my supplication. I poured out my complaints before him: and shewed him of my trouble. When my spirit was in heaviness thou knewest my path: in the way wherein I walked have they privily laid a snare for me. I looked also upon my right hand: and saw there was no man that would know me. I had no place to flee unto: and no man cared for my soul. I cried unto thee, O Lord, and said: 'Thou art my hope, and my portion in the land of the living. Consider my complaint: for I am brought very low.'

There was no one in the railway compartment when I boarded the train. Just before it started to move two men scrambled in. Out of breath, they tossed their coats and briefcases on to the luggage rack. Then they began to talk, at least one did, the other was strangely silent. Then he said, 'My mother died last night.' 'Oh,' came the reply, 'I'm sorry ... Do you think we shall win the Test Match this time?' And he elaborated his opinions. The other retreated into a silence which showed in his face. Clearly he suddenly felt alone, isolated in his personal grief. He wasn't with us in the carriage any more.

I feel sorry for people who are desperately poor, who suffer some nagging pain that won't go away, who have been made redundant, or who never get a holiday. What distresses me even more is people who have no shoulder on which to cry when such a tragedy as sudden bereavement hits them. Loneliness compounds sorrow. It breaks the heart. There are times in the lives of us all when we are brought very low. Sometimes we need someone to cry with us. Sometimes we need melancholy music. I am glad Psalm 142 is in the Psalter because now I know that God will not blame us if sometimes we are down in the depths. His is a shoulder on which we can cry.

A prayer

Lord, make me a sensitive person ready to sympathize, ready to listen.

Broken in heart

O praise the Lord, for it is a good thing to sing praises unto our God: yea, a joyful and pleasant thing it is to be thankful. The Lord doth build up Jerusalem: and gather together the outcasts of Israel. He healeth those that are broken in heart: and giveth medicine to heal their sickness.

Read verse 3 first, then verse 1. But can we praise God because he heals those who are broken in heart? Perhaps you have never had a broken heart. Perhaps you have never lost someone who is all the world to you and you wondered how you could ever live again. Perhaps you have never had a close friend and he/she has let you down. Perhaps you have never had a love affair and had to break it off because it 'wouldn't work'.

All these wounding experiences of heart-brokenness make you feel horribly alone. This is their terror. You are out on your own, a kind of outcast (see verse 2). You can't even talk about your feelings, for how could others enter into them?

But God provides medicine. No, not great theological explanations, not even sermons or uplifting books, probably not anyway. But the trees coming into leaf again, a budgerigar chirping to be fed, a child coming to show you a toy aeroplane, a day stumping across the hills. Nature is God's medicine, and simple things, and needy creatures wanting your help.

Mere pious talk? Don't tell me that. I think of a woman alone in Scotland, dying of leukaemia. The wild birds coming to be fed on her window-sill were her solace—*and this Psalm*.

Trapped

I cry with my voice to the Lord, with my voice I make supplication to the Lord, I pour out my complaint before him, I tell my trouble before him. When my spirit is faint, thou knowest my way! In the path where I walk they have hidden a trap for me. I look to the right and watch, but there is none who takes notice of me; no refuge remains to me, no man cares for me. I cry to thee, O Lord; I say, Thou art my refuge, my portion in the land of the living. Give heed to my cry; for I am brought very low! Deliver me from my persecutors; for they are too strong for me! Bring me out of prison, that I may give thanks to thy name! The righteous will surround me; for thou wilt deal bountifully with me.

Picture a grim cave in the forbidding rock foundations of Judea's mountain region, riddled with caves, haunts of wolves and jackals. David was in *one* of them, that was his only safety. His oppressors could not investigate *every* cave. His only hope of ultimate escape hung on this slender thread. Picture, if you can, David and his fellow desperadoes flattening themselves against the back wall of the cave every time footsteps broke the eerie silence outside.

But was the multiplicity of caves David's only hope? He thought so. Then he remembered God. Did he then bury his head in his hands and cry, 'Thou art my refuge and my portion in the land of the living'? Whatever the odds against, we are safe if in the line of God's will, as was baby Jesus, son of David, in the rickety manger cradle at Bethlehem with Herod glowering the background.

Prayer

Lord, I am at my wits' end today but I believe I am safe in your hands.

Notes from BRF

If you have enjoyed reading and using *Day by Day with the Psalms* you may wish to know that similar material is available from BRF in a regular series of Bible reading notes, *New Daylight*, which is published three times a year (in January, May and September) and contains printed Bible passages, brief comments, and prayers.

For further information, contact your local Christian bookshop or, in case of difficulty, The Bible Reading Fellowship, Peter's Way, Sandy Lane West, Oxford, OX4 5HG. Tel. 01865 748227. BRF is a Reg. Charity (No. 233280)